STORIES FROM *a Female* TRUCKER

80s - 90s

AF866258

PATTY ADAMS

Copyright © 2024 Patty Adams

ISBN: 9798989199549

All rights reserved. This book or any portion thereof may not be reproduced or used in any manner whatsoever without the express written permission of the author. Any similarities to real people are purely coincidental. Names and locations are changed to protect everyone.

A special thank you to a wonderful and talented lady named Sabrina, who did her magic and turned my manuscript into a book.

Created and first published, in 2024 in the United States of America.

Introduction

The women who started it all in the 1980s were less than a handful. We jumped into the male-dominated world of trucking headfirst, ready for the challenge. The work was hard at times, which made us strong and determined. Some days were often difficult, with brutal stereotypes that lasted a few decades too long. We kept our heads up and powered right on through it.

We give our heartfelt thanks to the people who were kind to us and who understood that we were out here just doing our jobs. Sometimes, it takes all of us working together to accomplish goals, and we did accomplish them.

Most of all, we had a blast and embraced the life of working as a trucker. Acceptance eventually came, and now many professional women are gracing our highways. The freedom of the open road was and still is amazing. I am so proud to have been one of the first solo women professional drivers. These are my stories.

~ ~

Chapter One

Maggie

I showed up for my 8 am interview a few minutes early. My heart beat a little faster in anticipation. It was important to make a positive impression. My current employment was ending because my boss was dying of a lung disease. I was already a trucker and excited for a new opportunity.

It was close to an hour's drive from my home. Finding a parking spot was easy. I maneuvered my Toyota hatchback right in front of the main building. This trucking company looked much like any other. I saw an office building, a repair shop, and a row of trucks and trailers parked in a gravel lot way behind the clutter of buildings. I wore jeans, work boots, and a new T-shirt.

A warm, brisk wind blew around my short brunette hair. There was a storm front pushing in from the west, making it a typical late September day in Indiana. I took a deep, nervous breath as I walked inside.

Four drivers were sitting at a table in the big open room just inside the door. Cigarette smoke hung heavy, and the room was dirty. They were talking and laughing, then dead silence when I closed the door behind me. The men sat there, staring at me with much curiosity.

"Hello, I am here to see Ron Anderson, the terminal manager," I asked politely.

Out of nowhere, a man's head popped out from a dispatch window nearby. He had to add his two cents. "We aren't hiring a cleaning lady, so get lost."

"Oh, never mind Brian over there," one guy said, ending in full-blown, exaggerated laughter. He slapped his knee, then coughed loudly. "He is our dispatcher." I was hoping to see him fall out of his chair and roll onto the floor.

"Well, okay, fine," I said, mildly annoyed. "Where can I find Mr. Anderson?" Then a moment later, an inside door leading into a hallway opened, and a middle-aged, slightly balding man greeted me. I noticed the bad comb-over.

"You are...?"

"Hello, I am Patty, and I have an appointment with you."

"Oh yeah, that's right." We walked a few steps to his office.

"Please sit down."

He offered me a chair; I sat down and noticed how small and dull his office was. Ron slid a three-page application across his desk in front of me, along with a pen that I handed back to him. I preferred to use my pen, so I grabbed it from my back pocket.

Ron asked, "Do you *really* drive?" He drew out the word 'really' as if I was only there to annoy him or sell him something. Then he added, "How far away do you live?"

I looked up from the application and made eye contact. His glasses are trying to slide down his nose, making his forehead look even taller. My eyes drifted up to look at his four or five glued-down hair strands. Stop staring, I silently told myself.

It's an hour's drive for me, and yes, I've been driving for the last eight months. I realize you are looking for at least two years of experience. I don't have that yet, but I handle the rig well. I will do a good job for you."

Ron looked hesitant. "Doubtful," he commented. "You look to be about sixteen. So, what has brought you to our company? What's the real reason?" I put my pen down and saw nothing much in his vacant brown eyes.

"I am twenty-six and single, in case you need to know. Steve is one of your drivers who I met at one of my fuel stops. He encouraged me to apply since my current job was ending. Steve said he would speak with you and put in a good word. We saw each other pretty often since our schedules were similar. He told me this is a good company to work for.

"Steve mentioned seeing a woman driver a time or two, and he said something about talking to you. Honestly, I expected a big burly woman with a Skoal ring and brown teeth. So, here I am with a teeny bopper pretending to be a driver." His tone was dismissive and rude.

"Why did you bring me all the way in here, Ron? How many women drivers have you actually seen or met?" I leaned back, crossing my arms tightly.

His look was vague. "None, I suppose. I was just assuming, but hey, I am always looking for good male drivers. Look, Patty, I will be the laughingstock of the industry if I hire you." Then, out of nowhere, he flipped the conversation.

"Do you have pictures?"

"What? What exactly do you mean by pictures?" His question shocked me, and I sat straight up, instantly on my guard.

Ron leaned back with his hands behind his head and said, "You are playing stupid with me. You know.... Pictures..." He said this over again slowly as if I were daft.

"What are you saying, Ron? You want nude photos of me?"

"Of course, I do. Smart girl," he said, staring at me.

"Sorry, those won't happen," I said, feeling angry that he had set up the interview and wasted my time. The joke was on me.

"Okay," he said, "No pictures, no job. I have just one more question. Do you do tricks?"

Screw the application. I quickly jumped out of my chair in anger and grabbed the door handle. I stood there for a moment, fluffed my hair, then leaned back in a dancer pose.

"Of course, I do tricks, Ron. My best trick is to stand up on two legs and tell you to go fuck yourself."

"Funniest thing I've heard today!" Ron said, as if I cared.

I quickly left the interview feeling humiliated, and to make things worse, I had to leave through the driver's room.

"Hey honey, come sit on my lap and give me a big smoochie," from the same table, minus one guy. I drove back home in a thunderstorm, thinking about how rude that company was. The heavy rain was a fitting end to a disappointing morning.

Two weeks passed, and my current job had ended. My phone rang, and it was Ron.

"I'm sorry, Patty; I overstepped my bounds when I asked for nude pictures." I was silent for a moment on my end of the phone. Ron was disgusting, and I wanted little to do with him.

"Yes, you stepped in it big time," I said coolly, leaning on my countertop, wishing I hadn't answered the call. I was about to hang up but couldn't help but wonder why in the world he would call me two weeks later.

"Can you come back in, and we will talk about putting you to work? I wasn't aware until I read your application that you did bulk work.

"So, what if I do bulk work? That sounds like a lousy excuse to hire me."

"Be here next Monday at 8 am for orientation," Ron said with an expectation in his voice. I hung up on him. The apology seemed superficial, and I certainly didn't like this man.

NINE MONTHS PREVIOUS

Mr. Stockton was a sick, tired old gentleman who placed an ad in the local newspaper, begging anyone to take the job. At least that was my take when I read it. I had taken a semester off from college trying to decide what career would suit me best, and I could use an adventure. I took a chance, a long shot, and called the number on the ad, and he asked me to come by the next morning to discuss the job. It was a record cold February.

"I can train you, no problem. How old are you, Patty?"

"I am 25, turning 26 next month." My fingers were sweating on the phone receiver in nervous anticipation.

"Close enough for horseshoes. How about coming in tomorrow morning bright and early, and we will go driving?"

"You mean a semi? You are going to teach me how to drive a truck?" I could barely contain my excitement. He responded after a terrible fit of coughing. Finally, he said, "You betcha."

I lived a few minutes away and was at his door at 7 am the next morning, complete with a new pair of work boots, work gloves, and wearing a pair of old jeans. It was so cold that day, single digits. I had put on a layer of thermals underneath my clothing, plus a knit hat.

Emmett's business was a Quonset hut in the middle of nowhere in northern Indiana. A tall man with messy clothes, a wafer-thin body, and brown hair welcomed me inside.

The first thing I noticed was a low-hanging light bulb crusted with a brownish-yellow film. Messy stacks of paperwork and trash were strewn all over his desk, piles of dirt everywhere, and the horrible cigarette stench was choking me.

Past all that, we hit it off immediately. Emmett's smile was sincere, and we took a liking to each other. I had a chauffeur's license, which was all that I needed. Well, except for a lot of training.

Emmett was a chain smoker, made clear by the giant overflowing ashtray as big as a bucket on his counter. Everything in his orbit, including himself, was nicotine-stained. "So, you need a driver?" I asked, trying to get the conversation started.

"Yes, I do," he said in a raspy voice as he crushed out a cigarette and then lit another. I was picturing his lungs thick with tar. He sounded awful.

"How did you ever become interested in trucks?" Emmett asked, curious.

"You look more like a high school cheerleader or preppie."

"No, I was never that. Think of me more like a square peg that never fits in. You know, the oddball, dyslexic screwball. I am my father's second daughter. My sister isn't into trucks and such things."

"Your dad drives a truck by any chance?" Emmett asked, interested.

"Yes, my dad is a trucker. How did you know?"

"Just a guess," Emmett winked, then added, "Oddballs fit right into trucking."

"Dad is encouraging me to follow in his footsteps. He spent years driving in the northern Minnesota environment. I spent my childhood listening to his stories about hauling hot tar and crude oil across harsh terrain. Winters were brutal there, bringing too much snow and temps often reaching 20 to 30 below zero. Dad moved us to the Midwest a few years ago. Past all that, I learned about mechanics, helping him repair cars in our garage. It's his weekend hobby. That officially makes me a tomboy, I suppose."

I was shivering in that poorly heated office.

"You are way ahead of most girls. How many do you know that could drive a truck? Or work on anything mechanical?" I didn't answer.

Emmett poured us each a cup of coffee, and I was happy to accept the steaming cup. It warmed my throat and his, too. We finished our cups, talking about the bitter cold day. Then, he lit another cigarette. I would bring my own coffee mug to his office after that day.

"A girl after my heart," he said, taking a long puff. I knew he meant the love of coffee, but I never smoked. Never.

"So, looking at your business, you used to have several trucks? I mean, you have about ten acres of nothing but gravel out there and a single-wide trailer to live in."

"You are perceptive, Patty. Yes, I owned a large company at one time. I sold everything off, and now I only have this one account. It's so bad I couldn't give it away. I am on the hook for one more year, and then I can retire for good.

Yes, I live right here. My wife passed away a good ten years ago, and I no longer needed a big house."

"I am sorry you lost your wife."

"Thank you. I get lonely, but that's life."

We walked outside into the bitter cold, negative something degrees. The truck was a frozen machine sitting all by itself behind a little building. Emmett introduced me to "Maggie." As we walked closer, I could see that Maggie was a day-cab truck with a long hood. Day-cab means no sleeper. The trucker lingo name for a truck like this is, 'a one stack Mack with a window in the back.' The gold bulldog hood ornament sat at attention. Emmett had parked Maggie next to a bulk trailer that looked like a giant insect. We both ignored the trailer for now.

"Maggie is a beautiful blue truck, but I see so much rust. She must be an old girl."

"Hush, she will hear you," Emmett said, startled.

"What?"

"Never mind. Yes, she is a 1967 R-Model Mack with a 237-horsepower Maxidyne engine. She will run circles around any other truck on the highway. She still has great power under that hood."

He reached inside the unlocked door and turned the key. Maggie sounded rough as the cylinders slowly roared to life. Black smoke billowed from her stacks. She shook and wheezed, struggling to come to life. It struck me that the truck and Emmett sounded the same. Finally, the engine smoothed out as she warmed. Maggie was dirty to the extreme. The doors popped and creaked on rusty, frozen hinges.

"Be careful getting in. The steps are icy," Emmett warned.

Maggie had torn seats, and the windows were so filthy and iced over that I could barely see out of them. I made a mental note that a bucket of hot, soapy water, Windex, and bleach would go a long way. Emmett groaned on old bones as he climbed into the driver's seat, situating himself. He pushed his grungy hair away from his eyes, tired eyes that no longer sparkled blue.

We waited a couple of minutes while the defrosters tried to melt some of the ice off the windshield, but not much melting happened. Cold, so cold. Our breath came out as icy fog. I could no longer feel my fingers or toes.

"She has a five-speed manual transmission, easy to shift. I had her fitted for power steering shortly after I bought her in the early 1970s. Armstrong steering is way too hard for an old guy like me, and you wouldn't have a chance," Emmett said, between terrible fits of coughing. I only nodded, frozen in the seat.

Emmett eased Maggie into first gear and showed me how poorly this truck handled with an embarrassing look on his face. She rode like a bulldozer, bumping and bouncing around his large gravel lot, as if on square wheels. I hung on for dear life as Emmett went up and down the gears, showing me how to shift. Fortunately, my car was a five-speed manual.

"I hope you can learn all of this. It's been so expensive for me to contract this run out." Emmett said with a hint of desperation. "My lungs are so bad. I can't add to my misery. Every driver I hire only stays a short time, and the fill-in company I am using is costing me a fortune."

The only thing I could think about was how cold it was and why Maggie didn't have heat.

"What on earth am I signing up for?" I asked, turning to face him in that frozen, filthy truck. Emmett slowed down and eased her next to his building. He pulled out the air brake knob while we were still moving just a little, which caused a sudden stop. I was jolted forward in my seat; I shot him a dirty look.

"Sorry about that. I need a driver to run up to Detroit to pick up salt pellets for a nearby water-treatment plant, three days a week."

"What's so hard about that?"

"It isn't hard, it's hazardous."

"Why would salt be hazardous?" I don't understand.

"You'll see. There is a large salt plume that comes up from underneath the trailer when you unload. You will understand better once we do the run together."

Emmet said, pulling a wad of cloth from his pocket. He held it close to his mouth and coughed up bloody mucous.

"That bulk trailer sitting over there?" I asked, cringing at the sight of his rag.

"Yes, exactly," Emmett said, then he backed up to the trailer. I heard a loud click as Maggie's fifth wheel grabbed hold of the trailer pin and latched tight. Emmett climbed out to crank up the trailer dolly legs and hook up the power and air lines. I watched him from Maggie's rear window. Emmett made sure he went over the hooking and unhooking procedures with me over the next few days.

We went around the block several times. Maggie rode so much better hooked up to the trailer. It was noon when Emmett had enough driving and called it a day.

"See you tomorrow?"

"Yes, for sure," I said, assuring him I was interested.

I would soon be a girl with a truck. I spent my free time cleaning Maggie and bringing her back to life. The first day was the only time I sat in the passenger seat. My training paid off. Within two weeks, I was comfortable driving Maggie with Emmett's teaching and guidance.

Finally, Emmett said, "Hey, Patty, you got this!" The best words I'd ever heard.

"How about fifty bucks per trip?" I knew the pay was meager but also that Emmett wasn't bargaining. "My offer is a fair wage for a young woman with no experience."

If I wanted to become a professional driver, I would have to shake hands with his offer. I had been working as a nursing assistant. They adjusted my hours to part-time and weekends to accommodate me. The only way I could afford my rent was to continue doing both jobs, at least for a while. I never discussed this with Emmett.

It was about 140 miles from Fort Wayne, Indiana, to Detroit to pick up the salt, then return and deliver the load to the water treatment plant. Emmett told me he had a fuel account already set up at an independent truck stop about halfway between here and there.

Emmett rode with me just once, my first trip up to Detroit. We loaded the pellets at the salt refinery, right on the scheduled noon appointment. Loading was easy.

After checking in at the guard shack, we drove slowly through the plant until we reached the loading bay for salt. A worker directed me to line the trailer up just underneath a large spout. There were three compartments in the trailer.

I would pull up to fill each one until the loading was finished. It took no time at all. The man doing the loading closed the trailer lids and sealed them.

After a brief wait, he handed Emmett the paperwork. He signed the top copy and gave that one back to the man. After that, we headed back to Fort Wayne for the delivery.

March temps were decent. Otherwise, we would have our coats on and blankets strewn across our laps. The temps finally evened out to normal in March. Still chilly but manageable. Emmett never explained why he wouldn't fix the heater.

"Skip the fuel stop today," Emmett said as we rolled through Ohio. He pointed out the fuel stop as we drove past. "I don't want to take the extra time."

"Okay," I said in agreement, but silently not agreed. Maggie could use some fuel, but it would have to wait. Emmett coughed up bloody lung material the entire trip. He was white as a sheet and wanted to get this day over with as soon as possible.

As we drove to Indiana, the afternoon was dragging on. We passed by freshly plowed farm fields and livestock barns, some of which had Red-Man tobacco logos. There were patches of lingering snow on the barren ground. Spring plowing and planting will begin soon. I enjoyed seeing the pastures of cattle and horses. Miles of fences lined the flat landscape. Emmett leaned toward me to give me instructions as we neared our destination. The water treatment plant was quite a ways inside the city.

After several traffic lights, he told me to turn right, then he pointed to a long building with a truck-sized pull through unloading bay.

"Pull straight into the building until the back of the trailer clears the door. This will center the trailer over the long grate on the floor. Set your brakes, then we wait for the receiver."

I set the brakes, and Maggie gave off the normal loud air discharge sound. The receiving clerk showed up within a minute to sign the paperwork and keep his copies. He climbed on top and removed the seals and he opened all three lids. After that, he disappeared through a side door.

"Listen to me close, Patty," Emmett said firmly. "Crawl way underneath the body of the trailer and open all three bottom drop doors as fast as you can. Hold your breath as long as you can."

"Alright," I said, not yet understanding how terrible this job was.

I crawled underneath the trailer and found the latches. I took a deep breath, then quickly released three-round ten-inch bottom drop doors in sequence.

Instantaneously, tons of pellets fall fast and hard down the grate, causing a giant plume of salt powder upward. Then I crawled out from underneath the trailer and ran to the cab, jumping back in as fast as I could. I gasped for air, huffing and puffing, just trying to breathe. I was covered in salt powder from head to toe. Emmett nods with approval from the passenger side. I clearly understand now why he can't do this job.

"You're kidding me, right?" We talked about how this run has nearly killed him. The salt emptied fast down the long grate, which spanned the entire length of the trailer. We were empty in 20 minutes.

Emmett's lungs were critical, but I knew he couldn't place the blame on just the salt. He smoked like a freight train running on old, dirty fuel. I knew my lungs were going to take a terrible hit, too. There was no way to avoid breathing this stuff.

Emmett explained that dust masks weren't beneficial because the salt pellets wear down to a powder in transit and almost instantly plug them up. There was no winning this war. We did the water treatment plant run together only once. It was clear in a hurry why this stuff was hazardous.

We were at Emmett's shop thirty minutes after unloading. I helped him out of the truck and got him safely inside his little trailer home. I eased him into a chair and placed a worn-out throw blanket over his lap. Yes, this was way above my pay grade, but he needed the assistance.

"Do you need to go to the hospital?"

"No, I will be fine, just need to rest a bit. Thanks anyway."

"Okay then, I am heading home. See you later, Emmett."

Time passed, and summer arrived. Maggie and I were having a blast, bumping and rolling down the highway despite the terrible unloading conditions. It didn't take long to discover that Maggie wasn't waterproof, either. When it rained outside, it rained inside, too. The biggest issue, besides no heat, was her state of disrepair.

Maggie's tires were smooth as bowling balls. Maggie also had noisy wheel bearings and a howl from the rear end.

Each trip, I would stop and top off the fuel and add at least a gallon of oil at the mom-and-pop truck stop Emmett had set up. An elderly couple owned this place and ran it themselves. Claire and Eddie put their heart and soul into their little truck stop, making sure the drivers felt welcome. They would prop the back door that led into the kitchen open in good weather.

Claire would keep an eye out for her regulars, then wave hello when we pulled into the fuel island, which was near the building. I would show up every other day about one-thirty in the afternoon, starving.

"I just made fresh chicken salad." Claire would holler within earshot from the back door.

"Sounds great!" I would holler back.

Claire would bring out giant sandwiches wrapped in wax paper along with cups of coffee and iced tea and pass the food out to those of us on the fuel island. Sometimes, it would be homemade soup or a big juicy cheeseburger. Her food was delicious.

I loved watching her short gray hair and apron blow in the breeze as she brought out the meal. She would always wear a casual dress with the hem way below her knees. Her support stockings would roll down and rest on top of her orthopedic shoes.

Claire had an old-fashioned charm and a million-dollar smile. The price was always $3.50, regardless of what the sandwich was. She never charged for the coffee, so each time, I would give her five bucks, a smile, and a big thank you. Everyone gave her big tips.

Eddie liked to be outside manning the fuel and gabbing with the men. He would occasionally walk past me, look at Maggie, and scratch his head in a fit of worry.

"Ya know, you gotta get that cheap boss of yours to buy some tires."

"Yes, and brakes and springs and bearings and winter heat. Would you like me to continue with this long list of needed repairs?" I said, laughing at the fantastic idea that Emmett was ever going to spend a dime. Then, I coughed, and wheezed, and coughed.

"It's not funny anymore, Patty. You are down to cords, and this is dangerous. I am not letting this go. I am awfully close to calling the D.O.T. and reporting your unsafe truck. You must realize this has been a scorching July so far. Tires blow much faster on hot days. It could save your life. Oh, and get that cough looked at."

"Ok, Eddie, I will talk to Emmett this afternoon. I know you are right, but Emmett isn't interested in bringing Maggie up to legal standards. He won't spend a dime to make her better. It's hotter than Hades in this truck, too, but that won't change either."

Just then, a driver-friend pulls in. His name is Steve. Eddie busied himself and walked away. I started into my sandwich and steaming coffee with the perfect amount of cream.

Steve was also a regular at Eddie's truck stop. We met soon after I took over this run. He was just as concerned as everyone else about the condition of Maggie. He pointed out the same things that Eddie was fussing over.

"Hi Patty, I see you're still driving that beater of a truck."

"Hi, Steve, yes, and you already know that my boss is dying of emphysema and whatever else. I am happy to report that Maggie is running better today than she has in a while. She didn't even need oil today, which is unusual."

I swallowed my last bite of chicken salad and washed it down.

"Between the rust and the bearings, hell, we can hear the racket from your truck before you pull in. That wreck of a truck drinks oil like there's no tomorrow and just look at that rusty frame! I hope he is paying you decent," Steve said, appalled.

"Hush, she will hear you," I said, halfway serious.

"What?"

"Never mind, he pays me $50 bucks a trip."

"Oh, no, no, no," Steve said, shaking his head. "That isn't pay; he is insulting you. Why don't you work for a better company? My company is looking for talented drivers. I will put a word in for you."

"I have little experience, Steve. It's doubtful your company would consider me. I appreciate the offer, but six months of experience isn't enough."

"Please think about it," Steve said, almost pleading.

I nodded, and then we both finished fueling and left. And I thought about it all the way back.

When I rolled into the shop that same day, I found Emmett in fantastic shape.

"Hi, Emmett. You look pretty darn good today."

"Thanks, the doc switched up my breathing treatments. Gave me something new to try, and it's helping me breathe easier."

"That's great news! You even have a bounce in your step." Pressing my luck, I asked. "How about a set of tires and an oil change for Maggie? She is getting dangerous to drive. Eddie is threatening me with the D.O.T."

"Eddie needs to mind his own business," Emmett said with a hostile glance. I realized right then that Emmett and Eddie weren't friends.

"Trucks are his business, too. He is genuinely concerned for my safety," I said, looking at Emmett, hopeful that he would agree.

"I have to figure out when to fit her in at the shop." It was more of a forced mumble than a sentence.

"That's a terrible excuse, Emmett. Why are you so grumpy today? You know I can't keep driving Maggie like this. The repair list is getting long. Her tires are down to cords." I felt angry and coughed again. My lungs hurt. Emmett ignored how I sounded.

"When my life ends, so will Maggie's." Emmett had no intention of fixing her.

Two days later, heading back from Detroit loaded, the inevitable happened. Maggie wasn't running right; I could feel an unusual tremor. I had a bad feeling and tapped her dash to coax her, "Come on, girl, get us back in one piece. Come on, Maggie."

I was still in Michigan, almost to Ohio, and heard a violent boom. Then, a half-second later, another boom just as loud. I jumped and cringed in my seat at the violent cannon-like booms the blown tires made. Both left rear drive tires had blown out.

The second tire blew because it was so thin it couldn't stand the pressure once the tire next to it was gone. I was fortunate that it wasn't a steer tire. That can cause you to lose control and slam into another vehicle and a myriad of other calamities. Luckily, nobody was near me. I eased the tractor and trailer off onto the shoulder and put my four-way flashers on.

Maggie left a mess of tire fragments all over the highway. Her engine didn't fail. It was the worn-out tires that couldn't take another mile of hot summer asphalt.

Maggie was toast as soon as the highway patrolman pulled up behind me and saw the mess. The blown tires took out the mud flap and bracket. The cracked springs were showing, along with the rust holes in the frame. Curls of smoke were coming up from Maggie's rear end. The rest of the tires were smooth, with cords showing.

The Michigan highway patrol officer stood behind the truck and shook his head. I climbed out of the truck and greeted him. The brisk July wind was in my face, and I could smell hot rubber.

"Hello, Officer."

"What are you doing driving this unsafe truck?" he asked with a mixture of authority and absolute disbelief.

"My boss refuses to fix it." All I could do was be honest.

"You aren't going anywhere! This junk of a truck is permanently out-of-service. I will call your boss and arrange for a wrecker to haul you back to your terminal. This truck isn't making another run, ever!" he hollered like a drill sergeant, to make his point clear.

He took down the information he needed to call Emmett. I waited two hours on the side of I-75 in Michigan. The wrecker finally showed up, and we exchanged hellos. His shirt said 'John.'

"I can't believe Emmett talked you into driving this old relic," John said, teasing me.

"How do you know Emmett?" John only grinned and fixed his ball cap.

I shrugged. "It's called paying my dues, I suppose. The girl with no experience gets to learn trucking. My trailer is loaded. Can your wrecker handle the extra weight?"

"Drop your trailer on the side of the highway. I can see that you are already away from the travel lanes. It will be fine sitting right there on the shoulder."

I unhooked from the trailer and pulled ahead far enough so John could line up his wrecker. Traffic buzzed past us as I helped him with the winch. We rode back together in his wonderful, air-conditioned wrecker, with Maggie in tow.

"You know Emmett is an asshole. I am his nephew, so I can call him that. This rattle trap truck should have been retired a decade ago. Hey, how do you like my new toy? My wife bought me this wrecker for my 35th birthday. My dad and I have a grain business, and as a side business, we started doing towing. It's been lucrative."

"Your wrecker is a beautiful piece of equipment. You have a smart wife who understands the business world."

"Yes, she does. Thank you."

After a moment, I said, "Maggie has been a dependable truck. She has done well since I took over this run. With all her problems, this is the first time I have been stranded."

John gave me a half-smile, then said, "Emmett must have talked to her."

"He sure did, and I talk to Maggie, too," I said, knowing there was a weird connection with no explanation. John adjusted his ball cap once again and smiled. After a long silence between us, I felt brave and asked about Emmett.

"There are many things Emmett keeps a secret that's none of my business, of course, but who is Emmett anyway? And why won't he do the basic repairs?"

John let out a long sigh. "Emmett had a big company at one time. He always drove Maggie when he needed to step up and help a driver finish a run or whatever the task was."

"I get that, but what happened?" I asked.

"One of his drivers killed a family in a van. Oh, this was about five years ago, give or take," John said, rubbing his chin like he wasn't sure how much to tell me.

He adjusted his ball cap once again, exposing messy hair. "They were probably heading to a fun vacation spot or who knows where. We'll never know."

"No way," I said, horrified. "Did he have a blow-out like I just did?"

"No, the word was he veered to avoid hitting a deer and lost control when he got into the loose gravel on the shoulder. He should have hit the deer. That family would still be here."

"That's awful," I said, feeling sad for the family.

"Emmett cost himself his own company. He was underinsured because he wouldn't spend any money. So, long story short, Emmett sold off everything except Maggie and the bulk trailer to pay the lawsuit. Emmett needed to keep this last contract so he could survive."

"Yes, he still needs to support himself," I said.

"True, but don't feel too sorry for Emmett; he is a miser in the first degree. This salt contract pays him well. It's you that's probably getting screwed."

"On a happier note, Maggie and I have been a pair since February, and she has held together until today," I said, trying to lighten things up.

A little over an hour passed, and we pulled into Emmet's place. On the door was a note: "Had a bad reaction to the new meds, went to the hospital. Emmett."

John and I looked at each other and then we looked over at crippled Maggie hanging off the wrecker hook.

"Now what?" I asked.

"I have a decent truck you can use until we can figure this out. My shop is a couple of miles away."

We went to John's place, and he parked the wrecker in the driveway, nosed up to the shop doors. I noticed he had a large brick truck shop with two bays and a lovely house close by. The driveway was concrete, and the landscape was perfect. A lot of pride went into their home and business. There were four grain trailers and three large silos behind the shop. They must have owned a big parcel of land for farming.

"Stay put," John said. He made a quick exit from the wrecker and disappeared inside the shop. A minute or two passed, and then John drove around with a much newer Mack. She was beautiful, shiny white with a silver bulldog on the hood. I jumped out of the wrecker and stood in awe.

I asked with curiosity, "What's the difference between the gold bulldogs and silver ones?"

"Oh, that's a great question. The gold bulldog means that they assembled the truck from 100% Mack components. The silver means it's a Heinz 57." We both laughed.

"She is a ten-speed, so it will be an adjustment, but I don't think you will have any trouble figuring her out."

John opened the truck door and helped me in. The truck was clean and new. John waved goodbye and walked inside his shop. The ten gears were easy to figure out; there was a pattern on the shift knob next to my right leg. She rode like a Cadillac, a dream of a truck, and everything worked like it was supposed to. I got spoiled in a hurry with air-conditioning and a plush interior. It was an easy drive back to Michigan. I retrieved my trailer with plenty of time left in the day to deliver the salt.

John kept Maggie for over a month while Emmett recuperated. Partly as a favor to me because July and August were too hot. I much prefer snow and cold. John made sure Maggie got some necessary repairs, including a set of decent used tires, even steers. Emmett groused about it, but he had no choice in the matter. John cleared up the rattle in the rear-end, and he must have done a bit of engine work because Maggie no longer sucked oil. Early September, Maggie and I were once again a pair.

John apologized for not fixing the heat for the upcoming winter months, saying that Emmett had capped the amount he could spend.

As grateful as I was for Maggie's improved condition, that state trooper in Michigan was firm about Maggie being permanently out-of-service, so I was terrified to drive through his section of the state. Worse yet, it would be winter again soon, and the thought of no heat until the contract ended next February was too much. Freezing to death and not being able to breathe was in my future. I had to derail this train.

I stopped by Emmett's office after my last run. It was the end of September, and I had enough of that miserable job. The rain ended about noon, making way for a sunny Friday. It was nearly evening when I finished my run and parked the equipment. I got caught behind a crash, and that had taken a while to clear up. Emmett was sitting at his desk with his eyes half-closed. I made a pot of fresh coffee and poured us each a cup.

Carefully, I set his cup on his crusty desk near his reach, not trusting his shaky hands. Emmett's eyes were dim, and his cough was worsening. He was so near death.

"Emmett, I want to thank you from the bottom of my heart for allowing me to learn to drive. Maggie and I had a blast. This job has taken a toll on me, so I am asking you if you can hire someone new to take over the final few months? For a while now, my lungs have been hurting; they are damaged and filling up with fluid. My doctor said that I needed to move on and heal. The inhaler he prescribed is doing a good job, and I am getting breathing treatments twice per week. They're helping, but I am a long way from healed. I can't continue doing this job, so I am giving you two weeks' notice. Also, you need to know that yesterday I had an interview at a small trucking company a little ways north of here, but it was a bust."

Emmett lowered his head and took a long-ragged breath; then he coughed in a long-wet sequence, catching a pool of frothy blood in his handkerchief.

"I knew this day was coming," Emmett said, slowly, with gravel and sadness in his voice, as he struggled to talk.

"The trucking industry is decades away from accepting women. I fear you will have problems, and very few will understand why this pretty young woman is driving a truck." He could barely get the words out. "There is real danger out there."

"Speak slow, Emmett, take your time."

Emmett stopped to take a ragged breath, followed by a cough and wheeze. Every breath looked painful. It broke my heart to watch him struggle.

"The industry refers to seasoned truckers as the old guard. These are intolerant men who don't want their final frontier spoiled by women, kids, or anyone they feel doesn't belong. Not every driver out there will give you a problem, but a few will give you many problems."

Emmett's speech was labored. He spoke very slowly. There was a death rattle in his words. I took a long drink from my cup while Emmett's coffee sat untouched. His lit cigarette burned down to ash on the tray.

"You don't understand how dangerous it is out there. I worry about you, Patty. You are naïve about trucking, and the lengths some men will go to take advantage of you.

You will quickly learn what I mean, and then you must protect yourself. The best thing you can do is limit what you tell someone during your travels," Emmett said sternly. Hard sweat was pouring from his ashen face.

It was abundantly clear that Emmett was worried about me. We have talked endlessly about this topic. I also knew with absolute certainty that this was no longer a two-week notice. This was the end of Emmett. He looked like a ghost. He was out of words and out of breath.

I wrapped my arms around his bony frame. "Thank you, Emmett, for all you have taught me, and for our many mornings together, drinking coffee by the pot full and laughing so hard. You have been a great friend; you will be in my heart forever."

He clutched me back as best he could in his frailty and whispered, "Goodbye Patty, it's been wonderful knowing you, and just know that you've been the light in my life for nearly a year. Follow your dreams."

I offered to help him into his trailer, but he said no, he wanted to be left alone. After one last look around, I shut off the coffee pot and left the light on over Emmett's desk. It cast an eerie yellow glow over the dying man. I softly whispered a forever goodbye to Emmett, then closed the door.

John's place was just a couple of minutes away. I needed to let him know his uncle was bad off. It was after 6 pm and I was happy to see a light still on, so I let myself in the side door. John was looking at a busted axle on one of his grain trailers. His shop was immaculate.

"That doesn't look good," I said.

"Oh, hi Patty, nice to see you."

"Hi, John, same here."

"I stopped by to let you know Emmett is very near death. I just left there, and I don't think he has much time left." My cough started back up right then. I couldn't help it. My lungs were so painful.

"Okay, I am glad you let me know. I will finish up and head over there. Does he need to go to the hospital?" John asked with a worried look. "Maybe you need a hospital?"

"He's beyond that point, and I'm getting treatments. I will be alright."

We just stared at each other for a moment, lost.

"How did the trailer axle get busted?" I asked, breaking the awkward silence.

John put his arms up over his head with a groan. He was upset and wanted to get it off his chest. He opened up like a flood.

"Well, Arnie and Anna are neighbors down the way a bit. They aren't a day under a hundred. Arnie was driving his Buick right down the middle of the road this morning, which, as you know, is barely big enough to be considered a two-lane. I was bouncing along with my grain trailer. The old coot has tunnel vision or no vision, and he is coming straight at me. He won't move over an inch. I didn't feel like a head-on collision, so I put my tractor right square in the ditch. Everything would have been fine if I hadn't caught the edge of the concrete drain with the trailer tire and ripped the axle. I had to pick the wrong spot, but he gave me no choice. Funny thing, Arnie puttered right past me, and he never noticed a thing. He was driving alone. Anna may have seen me had she been in the car, but it's hard to say."

"That's awful. You were empty, I hope."

"Yes, thank goodness. It would have been a nightmare to get this thing back home loaded. Fortunately, I had just unloaded at the mill and was heading home. I am really pissed off at Arnie, but it's kind of the same as being mad at a three-year-old for breaking a favorite toy."

I gave John an understanding nod.

"When you get a chance, can you please call me with an update? I will be home in a few minutes."

"Will do... oh, hey Patty, before you go, I want to take a moment and say thank you for sticking it out this long. The job was brutal, and we all knew it. And by the way, you were everything to Emmett. That reminds me, he and I bought you a gift a couple of weeks ago. Excuse me a moment while I go get it."

John came back with an oblong box all wrapped up. I opened the gift, and it was an ornate Italian switchblade knife. I gave John a surprised look. This knife was so beautiful. I was blown away.

"I am so touched that you both were thinking about me. A big thank you to both you and Emmett. You both bought me such an amazing gift. I will take great care of it."

"You know how worried Emmett was about your safety. We just hope and pray that you never need it." John showed me how to work it.

"Here is the release button. Be very careful, Patty. This knife would put any razor blade to shame. If you're not careful, this thing will take your hand clear off. It's a powerful weapon."

I practiced opening and closing it a few times. The long blade ejected at lightning speed, nearly jumping out of my hand. It would take time and practice to handle it properly.

It made John happy to watch me learn the knife. After that, it was time to go. John put his arm across my shoulders and then he gave me a good-luck kiss on my temple. We said our goodbyes.

My drive home was beautiful. I saw a brilliant full moon rising above a few red and purple ribbons left over from a gorgeous sunset. Emmett was ever-present in this amazing sky, and I took it as a good omen that I was going to make it in a rough and tumble boys' only industry. Barely two minutes after I got home, the phone rang.

"Hey Patty, just calling to let you know Emmett passed. I found him slumped over in his office chair. He was probably gone the moment you left him."

"Yes, I am sure you are right. At least he is no longer suffering. What happens now?"

"Emmett wanted to be cremated and placed next to his wife. We will honor his wishes. In the meantime, I need a big favor. There are a ton of things I have to wrap up and one of them to end the salt contract, but I can't do that before the load is due on Monday. I assure you I will cancel it after that. Can you run that load and then drop the trailer behind the silos and park the tractor next to the shop?"

"Yes, I can do that for you, but I prefer to use the white truck if you don't mind. The state police have warned me not to drive Maggie in Michigan. Somehow, by some miracle, I made it through this past month without getting pulled over and impounded."

"No problem at all. I will head over there later today to bring the equipment to my place and switch the tractors. Maggie needs to be put out of service anyway and set aside for auction along with the bulk trailer."

Monday came quickly, and I did my final salt run. John's place was dark when I finished up, so I said a silent goodbye and drove home. All that was left to do now was decide where to work.

~ ~

Chapter Two

Dirty Tricks, Practical Jokes, & Pranks

The day before Emmett passed away, I had an interview with a small trucking company. Ron, the manager, asked me for nude photos and basically called me a whore. He was disgusting, never giving me a chance at all. After two weeks of doing nursing assistant work with no trucking job in sight, I got an unexpected call from Ron.

He offered an apology and asked me to come and work there. I didn't trust him and needed some advice to decide if this job would be worth it.

My dad drove trucks too and he might be the perfect one to talk to. I had been wanting to go over trucking stuff with him for a while.

He was always home on Saturday, so I made a quick call to ask them if they had plans and if I could visit. They were happy to hear from me, so I made the short trip over to Ohio.

We talked about lots of things before and during dinner. Mom wasn't exactly thrilled with my career choice. She couldn't understand why a girl would love gears, the smell of diesel, and all things mechanical. She wanted me to be a nurse. At her request, I did two years of college studying nursing, science, and chemistry. Another year of school and I would have been doing state boards to become a registered nurse, but I really questioned if that was the career for me.

Mom fussed at me about dropping out of nursing school, and she was clearly upset. It was even more confusing to her because I had continued to work as a nursing assistant while driving for Emmett. She didn't know how little he was paying me; I didn't share that. She wanted more than anything to be a nurse herself, and I always felt she should have tried harder. She lived her life feeling short-changed, but without grudges.

According to mom, her parents said they couldn't afford to send her to college even though her father was an electrician, and they were better off than a lot of families. Women in the 1940s and 50s had few options. Mom had an awful time coming to terms with my decision and mentioned the big three career choices for women: nurse, teacher, or housewife. I acknowledged her, but I was happy to ignore that part.

We talked about Emmett and Maggie. Dad was angry that Emmett had me driving an unsafe truck, and he didn't understand why there wasn't a respirator issued.

"We tried respirators, but the salt grinds down so fine that it causes them to clog almost instantly," I said, in Emmett's defense.

Dad was glad to know I wore eye protection. I bought a pair of very necessary safety goggles soon after starting with Emmett. It was bad enough just breathing that stuff. I didn't need to go blind. I explained to my folks that my cough was getting better. The prescription inhaler plus several treatments were doing a good job of clearing out my lungs. The doctor was sure the damage wouldn't be permanent. I just needed time.

After dinner, I got the chance to bring up my job interview and how rude Ron was. Dad shocked me with his answer, and I think looking back that he didn't really understand just how bad that interview was.

"Listen Patty, Ron was probably testing you to see how much you would let him dish out. You may have just read too much into it. Maybe he is a big joker and meant nothing by it. The important thing you need to realize is that you have so much to learn from the men.

Listen to them closely, follow their lead, and always walk three steps behind them to show respect. Know your place. You are already on your way to becoming a professional driver."

"I am polite and respectful. He wanted nude pictures!"

Dad let out a whoop-whoop belly laugh. That caught me off guard, and I wasn't sure what else to say. Mom and I just looked at each other momentarily. I could read her thoughts.

"Mom, I don't think nursing is the right career for me, and women have more choices than your big three. I am sorry. It may take you years to understand, and you might never. This career choice makes me happy. I don't fit into normal girlie jobs."

"Look Pat," Dad said, before Mom could rebuttal, "Just take the driving job and walk away from nursing. I know that you will be just fine. You can handle yourself."

It was getting late and time to go. Dad wanted to tell a story. He would often repeat stories, and we would always pretend like it was the first time hearing it. The one he loved to tell was the time he ran with a woman driver pulling a flatbed with a tall load of something or other which could easily cause the rig to become unbalanced.

He followed her across Illinois and Missouri. According to the story, she started out as an owner-operator team with her dad in 1975, but he got sick and could no longer drive. She took over the family trucking business and was doing it alone. He admired her skill and let her know how impressed he was with her skill and courage. They chatted the miles away until one or the other needed to exit off and carry on.

In the early years, women drivers were running as teams with men, usually their husbands. The industry gave very few women credit or even a chance at all. We were called seat covers, truck sluts, lot lizards, diesel dikes and tacos. Women drivers were chased, grabbed, sworn at, and belittled, but that didn't hinder us. We worked through those years proud to be truckers.

Dad would talk about how trucks were built for work and not comfort. Windows and door seals wouldn't do squat for keeping the rain and cold out. Everything rattled, shuttered, puttered, or groaned. Dad ran on springs and inner tube tires, which eventually were replaced by non-tube tires and air bags to support our axels. We talked about extreme temperatures up north and diesel number one, which is actually kerosene. Diesel number one did the job of helping to keep trucks rolling. Truckers had to use it to keep fuel from gelling and causing them to be stuck on the shoulder of the road until help could arrive.

Dad went on about this and that and then we said our goodbyes. I thought it would be best if I didn't show my parents my fancy new switchblade. My mother would have come unglued. My new toy stayed home.

Monday morning came, and I showed up for orientation, much to Ron's amazement. He had a big grin, then he pulled me into his office and apologized once again.

"Okay, I forgive you Ron. By the way, what does this silly job pay? You never went over any of that with me."

"Oh, I never had the chance to tell you. We pay 0.21 cents per mile and $10 dollars for each stop and $10 per hour for detention after 2 hours. Our drivers average 2500 to 3000 miles per week. You'll get two days of orientation, then you'll each be given a truck and you'll be ready to go."

"That's a huge pay increase. I think I made the right decision."

Orientation wasn't much. It amounted to two other guys and me. The first day was going through company policies and paperwork. Ron explained they would pay drivers from the info we wrote on our run sheets. This is paperwork where we list our pickup and delivery points, and there is a second sheet where we list each state line.

We list our beginning and ending mileage plus the mileage of each state line we cross so the company knows how much fuel tax to pay each state.

Many states would require a diesel purchase to help offset the tax burden owed by the trucking companies. These were the years before IFTA, or the International Fuel Tax Agreement was put in place and simplified all of this. Ron issued us a couple of logbooks and a fuel card for the truck. He made sure we understood the company policy about logbooks "Always make the company look good." I didn't know what that meant, but it would become clear in no time.

Ron introduced us around the terminal. We met Brian, two office women, Eleanor, and Lisa, and then a safety guy named Harold, who cared little about safety. He was just interested in what the women were wearing, and if he got to peek at something. I saw that immediately when Harold bent over and cocked his head to look up Lisa's dress as she walked past him.

Harold looked at Ron, "Can you and Patty step into my office for a moment?" The two guys stayed back.

"You realize you are the first woman we have ever hired, right?" Harold stared at me, making me feel incredibly uncomfortable. Then Brian came storming in uninvited and Harold let him stay.

"Yes," I answered.

"I am going to make this clear to you right here and now. The first day you open your mouth about sexual harassment will be the last day you drive a truck.

For us or anyone else. I have the power through DAC to blackball you in the industry."

"That sounds a little extreme, don't you think?" Ron said.

"We can't have troublemakers working here," Harold snapped back.

Brian shot me a big, nasty grin and left Harold's office.

"Who decided I was going to make trouble? All I want is a driving job." My cough started up again. "I am sorry for coughing."

"You aren't qualified to work here if you are sick," Harold said.

"Get off her back, Harold. She will be fine. I trust her to do the job." Ron said, defending me.

"You're both excused."

Harold was creepy.

I looked at Ron in the hallway, "What does DAC mean?"

"It stands for Drive-A-Check. It's something new and considered a rap sheet for professional drivers. Everything good and bad can be recorded on DAC. Say, for instance, if a driver abandoned the equipment or quits without notice. That would go on his or her DAC report. Employment history, drug use, and just about everything else can go on the DAC report."

"What if something is false in the report?"

"Good luck getting it fixed. That would amount to a court hearing and the driver usually never wins."

"Well, that doesn't seem very fair."

Ron ignored that comment, and the two other guys in orientation soon caught up with us. We went outside to the repair shop to look around. Jimmy was the daytime mechanic, and we all said hello. That shop was a far cry from John's, but probably typical for a trucking company. There was grease and oil pooled on the floor, tools and parts strewn all over, and a dirty engine smell. We didn't walk past the doorway.

As we walked back into the office building, Ron reminded us that Brian was the head dispatcher. Brian had seen me before. Of course, about a year ago, when I was told they weren't hiring a cleaning lady. It made no difference because he wasn't having any part of a woman driver. He made sure I knew with absolute certainty that women belonged at home and my short stay would be a guarantee.

"You won't make it past your first run," was a promise that my job would be a challenge.

I met a few other drivers that day like Gabe who was fun to talk to. He was all about his boat and looking forward to his two-week summer vacation out on Lake Michigan.

He told me all about his pride and joy, which was a 1979 Viking 43-foot yacht with twin Detroit Diesel 671 engines. She has plenty of living space and all teak interiors.

Adam was much quieter, reserved, and polite, and he had nice things to say to everyone. His personal life didn't come up too much, so I can't say for sure if he was married or not, but that didn't matter. He was there to work, and he minded his own business.

Steve, who I met doing the salt run, is a single carefree guy about the same age as me. Nice guy, average and polite, but nothing too remarkable, just a regular guy. There was Marty, who seemed shy and Shorty, who was about six foot five.

We were all just truckers doing our jobs. I would eventually meet everyone. Fifteen drivers worked here. So far, the few I've met were all polite. This quickly changed.

The next morning, before going to the terminal for day two of orientation, I packed my bags, knowing I would go out on a run. I walked into the orientation room and saw only one new driver sitting there. His name was Jeff. The other guy didn't come back.

Jeff and I were each assigned a truck. This company had cabover Freightliners with five-speed Eaton-Fuller manual transmissions, Cummins diesel engines, and center point steering. This means you needed a lot of arm strength to turn the wheel, especially with a loaded trailer.

Center point steering is difficult to explain. It was a short-lived option for trucks. It was only a notch or two better than Armstrong steering and nothing near the ease of power steering. It worked with the front axle for maneuverability. It was a train wreck for handling and was a serious adjustment for me since I had not built-up that kind of arm strength yet. The Freightliner assigned to me was at least fifteen years newer than Maggie. It didn't have a hood. Cabovers are like driving square boxes down the road.

It would take me a while to adjust to driving a cab-over, so much different from a truck with a hood. Most of all, I would miss seeing a little bulldog sitting on the hood guiding the way.

Mack's are different of course than Freightliner's, but in the end, trucks are trucks. I had a single size bunk, a doghouse, and a passenger seat. A doghouse is a hump between the driver's seat and passenger seat. It's an engine cover, so to speak, but you don't remove it. The engine sits directly underneath the cab and the cab is jacked forward from the back to work on the engine. I had side boxes for tools and junk that opened with a tug of a cable inside the driver's door. Trucks all vary widely for interior space and comfort.

Day two of orientation was a bunch of nothing. A few more drivers came and went, offering introductions and welcomes. The men were polite guys who were more than a little curious about why I wanted to drive a truck. Not a single rude comment from anyone, yet. We wrapped it up about noon and then I went shopping for supplies.

I bought cleaning spray, a roll of paper towels and a wind-up alarm clock, a six-inch ruler for my logbook and bedding.

It was a chilly day with a brisk wind. I spent close to an hour cleaning up the truck interior and windows, about half freezing to death while wiping everything down.

Ron walked outside to find me and suggested I stay at the company hotel next door. It was there primarily for the drivers to use, free of charge.

"No thank you, I don't live that far away."

Ron quickly said, "You need to be here at 6 am, so this will save you from getting up so early." Very reluctantly, I stayed at their hotel and slept terribly.

The heater barely cranked out enough heat and rattled like an angry entity possessed it. I was restless, not knowing what Brian was planning with my first dispatch. The room was clean enough but had a noticeable trace of cigarette smoke and the minimum amount of things necessary for a plain hotel room. The alarm buzzed at 5 am. I rolled out of bed, knowing I hadn't slept much at all. I was thankful the water was hot for a shower.

Was signing up to work here a good idea? Maybe I hadn't tried hard enough to find something better. Most trucking companies want at least two years of verifiable experience. Okay, I am nowhere near that. I needed to be more appreciative to Ron for the opportunity he had presented to me and do my new job the best I could.

It's 5:40 am. I left the hotel and drove the short distance to the terminal. It was a dark, cold Wednesday morning. I was on time for my 6 am dispatch. I put my clothes and bags in the truck and started it up to let it warm. After that, I parked my car and walked inside. I remembered Brian didn't come in until 7 am. My day was instantly better.

The night guy looked through the dispatch window and introduced himself.

"Hello, I am Larry. Welcome to the company."

"Hello Larry, nice to meet you. Thank you for the nice greeting."

"You're welcome. I printed your dispatch out and put it in your box. It's about halfway down the row. I think you will enjoy working here." Larry said with a friendly smile.

"I hope so. I really like everyone so far." I was careful not to mention Brian's promise.

My paperwork box was easy to find, and I noticed that someone taped my name over another driver's name. Some guy is talking behind me.

"Hey new girl, I heard Ron hired some fresh meat for us guys." He was laughing at his own comment.

"Shut up and play nice, Roger," Larry said, who was in earshot.

I introduced myself. "I am Patty. Nice to meet you."

"Hi Patty, I am Roger!" He was enthusiastic. "Hey, nice tits!"

"Not cool, Roger," I shot back, and sat down to read my dispatch. Skinny Roger, with his hat tilted a little sideways, leaned over my shoulder.

"That's an easy run. You are only going two hours down the road to unload and then come straight back empty."

"You have been to this place?" I asked.

"Yes, I sure have. The load is palletized, and the customer is a warehouse that unloads us as soon as we get there." Roger gave me directions. The trailer was loaded and sitting in the back lot.

"Make sure you verify the trailer number, and the seals match the bills, then hook up. That run is a piece of cake." Roger said, being helpful.

My truck had warmed up enough to drive. I sat still for a few minutes, looking over the gauges. Everything about the truck was different.

Time to go. I exhaled slowly, then gently eased the transmission into second gear, noticing the clutch was a little stiff. The engine purred as I slowly crept along the gravel lot to the row of trailers and found mine.

The loaded trailer was easy to find. I slowly backed up underneath it until the pin snapped in place, locking the tractor and trailer together. I did a quick tug with my tractor to ensure the pin was secured.

I got out and hooked up the two air lines to the trailer, paying attention to the proper color coded glad-hands, red for emergency air and blue for service air. Then, I plug in the electrical cord to the trailer for lights and crank up the trailer legs, or dollies, as they are called. The pre-trip inspection was next in the pitch dark, which amounted to checking the lights and tires on both the tractor and the trailer. Also, I checked the seals which must match the bill of lading. I had already checked my water and oil yesterday afternoon during the time I was cleaning it.

The truck felt good as I drove slowly across their large lot. It's not struggling under the weight of the load. That's a sign of a good truck. My nervous bladder felt full, so I stopped at the office for a moment before leaving. After all that, I jumped back into my warm, idling truck just to realize my brakes wouldn't release.

This makes no sense; my rig was working perfectly. I felt embarrassed and frustrated because I couldn't figure it out on my own. The shop was open, so walked over and explained my problem to Jimmy.

"Seems to me someone played a practical joke on you, Patty."

We walked out to my truck, and he found the problem in two seconds.

"Someone switched your air lines. Your brakes won't release if they are hooked up backwards."

"It had to be Roger," I said, annoyed. "He was the only driver I saw this morning."

" That sounds about right," Jimmy said, as he put my air lines back where they belonged. "Roger is a big joker around here, so just take care and always look at your air lines and make sure you are hooking them up properly."

"By the way, don't trust some of these guys around here. You are the first woman we have ever hired, and a handful will give you trouble."

"I hooked them up correctly, thank you."

Jimmy shot me a dismissive glance as he walked back into the shop.

Roger gave me perfect directions. I showed up at the customer a half hour before my 9 am appointment. I parked the truck near the docks, walked inside, and found the receiver. He greeted me with a friendly hello.

"You must be new. I have never seen a woman driver for this company before and we get a load from your company twice a week." He was grinning and shook my hand.

"Yes, this is my first load with this company."

"Back into door three."

"Okay," I answered, then walked back out to the truck to get it backed in. I lined up about twenty feet from the dock to open my trailer doors. The receiver hollers from the dock to tell me to break the seal. I cut the seal, then opened the trailer doors just to see a disaster. There are hundreds of cases of cooking oil all stacked on the floor. Not a single pallet to be seen.

Brian planned this on purpose so I would have to pick up and hand stack the entire load of cooking oil, knowing that I don't have the strength or stamina for a task that huge. This is an impossible job for one person.

The receiver saw this too when he looked directly into my trailer from the dockside. He looked angry. I finished backing in and joined him on the dock to discuss this.

"We have a problem here," the receiver said.

"The dispatcher promised me I wouldn't be working here past my first day."

"I really dislike your dispatcher, Brian. We have banged heads frequently. Do you want to work for these people?"

"Yes, I am stuck for the next two years until I get enough experience to work for a better company, and I hope a better company exists."

"Yes, they sure do. Let's show Brian you can't be pushed out this easily. I will get a bunch of workers in this warehouse to pitch in and help. We will have this trailer unloaded in no time flat."

I lit up, "You would do that for me?"

"You bet I will. I hate Brian that much. I will charge him for our pallets, too."

So, that's just what happened. A dozen of us worked together and had that trailer emptied and swept out in less than two hours.

The receiver gave me a hearty handshake and a grin when we were done. He was so pleased to ruin Brian's plan. I expressed my thanks to him and the others who lent a hand. We were all dirty, sweaty and tired from unloading the nasty load that was supposed to intimidate me into quitting. I will be forever grateful for that amazing gift of help.

The speed of unloading that trailer gave me time to stop and wash the dirt off my face and hands and grab a quick sandwich before rolling into the terminal at exactly 2 pm.

I dropped the empty trailer out back in line with the other trailers. I parked my tractor and walked into the building. Brian saw me walking across the lot after parking the truck and he wasn't happy. He was screaming as I walked into the driver's room.

"You can't bring back a loaded trailer!"

"I didn't bring back a loaded trailer. It's empty and swept out."

Brian was shouting, "You could NOT have unloaded that entire trailer and be back this soon!"

"Well, I did exactly that. Go look for yourself."

"Fine, then!" he said while slamming things around his little dispatch office. "I have nothing else planned for you to do right now."

"Good, I am going home. Call when you have another load for me."

Brian pouted the entire week. He didn't dispatch me until the following Monday morning. He called to tell me I was dispatched to pick up a load of canned food that would be delivered to a food warehouse near Carlisle, PA at 7 am Tuesday morning. I drove straight to work, packed my truck, and started it up to de-ice the windshield. I walked into the driver's room to retrieve any paperwork from my box. The same four men I had seen during my interview were there. Every driver I have met so far has been polite. These guys weren't. They were rude and obnoxious. One at a time, they introduced themselves. Mark, Leroy, Bill, and of course, Roger, whom I had previously met. These guys were a rag-tag group of guys wearing flannel shirts, jackets, and muddy boots. Nothing remarkable about them. Bill looked and smelled like he could use a shower and deodorant. Bill and Mark immediately start in, "I sure feel hungry for beaver stew," and "Hmmm, yea, maybe she will let me have some of that."

"Go out with me Patty," Bill said.

"I am not interested. Don't ask again."

"Why not? You're cute."

"Leave me alone. Besides, you smell terrible. Don't you ever wash? And for the record, I won't date the men I work with."

The comment went right past him. He just grinned. Mark said something about "shoving his missile up my rocket socket." I was supposed to be shocked, but I wasn't. I let the remark slide right off my back. Leroy adjusted his thick glasses. He was a short, round guy with dark greasy hair. He looked highly embarrassed, rocking on one foot, then the other. Then he stared at the floor, not saying a word.

These guys were laughing and snorting, trying to get the best of me. Without missing a beat, Roger speaks up, "I lost my phone number. Can I have yours?"

Brian was laughing himself nearly to tears.

"Oh, hey Roger, that was so nice of you to switch my air lines the other day. Consider it once and done." He adjusted his hat and cleared his throat while his buddies laughed and chortled obnoxiously.

"Good one Roger! You showed her who's boss!"

Leroy, who was embarrassed, said nothing as he pushed past me right out the door, quickly heading to his truck. There may be hope for Leroy.

Emmett had prepared me, and it turned out he was spot on accurate about the trouble I would have with a few.

~ ~

Chapter Three

Meeting Carlos & More Problems Fitting In

The heater in my truck worked great; such a treat to work in comfort. I did a pre-trip inspection. Brrrr, that wind was icy. I zipped my jacket and put my hood up. The company parking lot had been plowed after several inches of snow had fallen overnight.

A patch of ice caused me to lose my footing, and I bounced off the rear of my trailer, catching myself on the ICC bumper. Another driver came running over to help me up.

"Are you okay?" His voice was pleasant. I looked up and saw a big guy ripped head to toe with muscles. I was hoping he was as friendly as he sounded.

"Yes, I think so, but I am feeling a little awkward."

"Please don't feel that way and by the way, my name is Carlos. I started driving for this company about a year ago."

"Pleasure to meet you, Carlos." I am quickly on my feet.

"Are you sure you are alright?"

"Good as new," I said and thanked him. "At least you aren't making horrible comments to me right now."

"You must be talking about those guys that hang out in the driver's room. Try your best to steer clear of them."

"Most definitely. By the way, Carlos, do you like working here?"

Carlos looked happy. "The job is better than what I had. I came here looking for better pay. The company I was with was only paying $0.15 a mile and I was having a hard time supporting my wife and twin girls. There were other issues too."

"You have twins?"

"Yes," Carlos said proudly, "Belle and Holly, they are four years old and the pride of my life." He was beaming.

"Christmas babies!"

"Absolutely."

Carlos wanted to talk more, so we hung out for a few minutes.

"Do you know why ICC bumpers exist?"

"I don't have the first clue," I answered, eager to learn something new.

"Late June 1967, actress Jayne Mansfield was traveling with her driver and attorney friend through Mississippi in the middle of the night. They were heading to New Orleans for a show the next day. The county near Biloxi was doing mosquito fogging which obscured everything - including the truck in front of them. Her driver slammed into the back of that semi, killing all three adults in the front seat. Jayne's head was smashed to bits and almost completely severed. Three of her five children were with them asleep in the back seat. They all survived. The trucking industry knew they had a big problem with decapitations caused from rear-end collisions. Jayne was one of many casualties. The invention of ICC bumpers goes a long way to help rear-end collisions from being fatal."

"That's the most horrible thing I have heard in ages." I shivered with that gruesome picture in my head. We both stood quietly for a couple of moments. We're done talking after that and say goodbye.

It was a several-hour drive to Carlisle and beautiful. The landscape was a bit hilly, with dense trees and rocks lining the highway. It must have taken years of hard work to build the toll road. Rocks needed to be blasted out and tunnels carved through the mountains, along with miles and miles of concrete and asphalt. It was something new to experience. The entire highway through lower Pennsylvania was truly an engineering feat.

My directions were good, and I arrived at the food warehouse later that evening for my 7 am appointment. There was enough room to fit my rig in between a couple of other trucks parked in the waiting area. I was glad to take off my boots and settle in for some sleep. A knock on my door woke me up an hour before my appointment.

"Tell the driver to back into door five," said the face in my window.

"Okay," I answered groggily, without trying to explain that I was the driver.

My education came fast about what food warehouses were all about. Big wood, small wood (pallets). All the neatly palletized cases from the shipper had to be broken down and counted, re-stacked, staged, and tagged for the receiver to put away on their tall shelving. In most food warehouses, the driver does the unloading and sorting out and re-stacking the cases of goods on additional pallets. This hard, exhausting work put on the backs of drivers. I learned that 'lumpers' are for hire to do the work for the driver. Some companies won't pay for that service, including the company I was working for. Drivers have to reach into their own pockets if they want to hire help.

Other companies happily pay for the lumper service, knowing their drivers can sleep for a few hours and be ready for their next dispatch. This load was grueling work. I had to re-stack the entire load of canned food on shrink-wrapped pallets onto little warehouse pallets called small wood or half sized pallets. They are small on purpose to fit on warehouse shelving. It was a four-hour job of bending and stacking cases of canned food.

The receiver jumped in and helped me, and a couple of nearby drivers offered to help. The work was still very hard, and my back ached so badly after all that. I wasn't strong yet, just a slender young woman who had so much to learn and a lot of strength yet to build up. Within a few weeks, and many loads requiring breaking down and re-stacking, my arms became stronger, and I had better stamina. Not every load was bad, and some were worse. Brian made sure I got at least one load every week that required breaking down.

Heading back was interesting and a little weird. I stopped for fuel at a truck stop just across the Ohio line on my way to a company in Cleveland, Ohio, where I was to make a pickup later that same day. I didn't have a list of the fuel stops we could use or if a list even existed. Up ahead was a sign for a fuel stop coming up at the next exit, and the truck ahead of me had the same plan. We backed down our speeds, and I followed him down the exit ramp. The fuel islands were busy, so we each pulled behind trucks already fueling and waited our turn. The card readers at the pumps weren't invented yet, so to get fuel, a driver had to go inside the truck stop and wait in line at the fuel desk to get approval to buy fuel. Not really a big deal, just time consuming.

This truck stop was much like every other truck stop out there, a fuel desk on one side and across the room there are rows of shelves lined up with petroleum items like oil and fuel additives, window washer fluid and all sorts of truck junk. The place had a dirty floor from melted snow and tracked in mud. The far side of the building was a restaurant with the clang of dishes echoing through the place. It was finally my turn at the fuel desk and a woman was working by herself. She was somewhere in her mid-fifties, trying her best to reclaim her youth.

The first thing I noticed were her earrings. They were an inch square pair of dice hanging down from her ears that dangled as she walked. Her hair was big and over- teased, looking like a large beehive sitting on her head. She layered her face with too much make-up.

She wore a pink blouse that was cut too low with her boobs pushed up way high. Her name tag said Eunice, and I could tell right off the bat she was born to do that job. It was finally my turn at the counter.

"Hello, can you please check my fuel card to see if I can buy fuel here?"

She wasn't having any part of it.

"Oh honey, you just run along, yer upsettin' my customers."

Half a dozen drivers are standing in line staring at her pushed-up boobs.

"Upsetting who?" I asked.

"Well, all my men, that's who." She turned to help another customer.

"I really need fuel, please."

"Now I have had just about enough of you, miss who-ever. Now get yourself long gone outta here before I call someone."

The driver standing next to me came to my rescue.

"She is a driver. She got off the exit right behind me and pulled in behind the truck in bay five, and I am directly next to her in bay four. Can you please check her fuel card?"

She gave me a big, exaggerated eye roll and checked my card. "Yep, you can get fuel. I turned pump five on. Make it quick."

"Thank you," I said to the driver who rescued me.

Eunice was quickly flirting and laughing with someone else. Big hoots and howls, overly dramatic and obnoxious. Her turf, absolutely.

It was too much for Eunice to just leave well enough alone. Right in the middle of getting fuel, a county sheriff's deputy pulls up and blocks me on the fuel island. I don't stop fueling to talk to him; I make the officer walk over to me.

"I got a call from the fuel desk that you were making trouble."

"Really? How much trouble does it cause to ask for fuel?"

Officer Clarence Mains looked uncomfortable standing near me with his belt fastened two notches too tight, trying to hold an extra thirty pounds of belly fat in place.

"So, who called you? Eunice?" I asked, and he looked surprised that I knew her name, not remembering that she wore a name tag.

"Do you know Eunice?" he asked, fumbling with the question.

"Not as well as you must know her," I said, smiling.

Officer Mains stood up tall, hiked up his pants up and snuffled.

"Yes, ma'am, she does love us men!"

"I bet she does!"

Officer Mains found himself lost for words.

I had finished fueling by then and placed the nozzle back on the pump and shut it off.

"May I go now, Officer Mains? I have to be in Cleveland later today."

"Well, I suppose nothing much really happened here. Yes, you may leave."

The rest of the trip was uneventful. I got a nice surprise when I pulled in and discovered the company where I was scheduled to pick up a load was closed until 7 am the next morning. The mom-and-pop truck stop nearby had a few open spots. I badly needed a shower and a meal. A good night's sleep gave my sore body a chance to recover. Although I woke up the next morning feeling like my truck had run me over about seventeen times.

I was careful not to call in until after I had picked up the load the following morning. Brian said nothing out of line when I gave him an ETA of 1 pm back to the shop.

The load of cut metal sheets were staged and ready, making it easy for a dock worker to load the trailer. I rolled out of the customer by 8 am - feeling great.

Brian was waiting for me when I got back. I dropped the loaded trailer in the yard on the pad. The fifth wheel pin didn't pull as easily as Maggie's, but a single hard tug did the trick for unhooking. I walked inside with no clue what was being planned.

"Patty, I am sending you to Paterson, N.J. leaving out Thursday. You are going to run out there with Mark. You and Mark can coordinate what time to leave. Patty, your delivery appointment is midnight in Paterson, N.J., and Mark, your appointment is 2:30 am in Bridgeport, Connecticut."

Of course, Mark was standing right there at the dispatch window near Brian, ready to help me find the east coast. Completely unnecessary.

Mark's hair was shiny clean and pulled back in a ponytail. His matching chocolate eyes made him a handsome fellow. He had high cheekbones that made him look Indian, but his vulgar mouth stripped him of everything nice or handsome. He ran his fingers through his ponytail, twisting it around.

"My load is delivering just after yours, but I have to go up to Connecticut, so once I get you squared away, I will finish my run."

"What time are we leaving out?" I asked.

Mark looked over at Brian, who filled in the blanks.

"Both loads are fresh boxed meat coming in from Nebraska and the loads will be here very early tomorrow morning."

"Will the loads be here by 4 am?" Mark asked.

"Yes," Brian said, not looking up as he shuffled through some other paperwork.

Mark sat down at a table and was busy figuring out mileages.

"Patty, you have about 730 miles to your destination, which means about 15 hours of driving, and I have about 820. I must deal with New York City. You got the better deal."

"Go home and sleep. We need to leave out exactly at 4 am tomorrow morning. We both have some hard driving ahead of us. Unless you want to stick around and test out something else hard?"

"You are a disgusting person, Mark, and I am not looking forward to this. I can find New Jersey on my own without your help."

"No such luck. I was instructed to babysit you." Mark said with a smirk.

Both men laughed as we walked out the door. Brian ran to the door to shout something at Mark.

"Don't forget what we talked about."

Mark waved his hand to acknowledge something between them.

It was still early in the day, so I made plans to go home and call a good friend whom I haven't seen in a while. She picks up on the first ring and agrees to meet me at a local dive for dinner. She gets there first, and we give each other a big hug before getting situated.

"How is that new trucking job going?" Avery asked as we sat down in the corner.

"Great so far, just a few ups and downs, just trying to get used to everyone."

We order burgers, eat, laugh, and let off steam. The place was buzzing with activity.

"Are you still doing bookkeeping for that garden shop? And your husband, Jack, is he still in construction?"

"Yes, we both have decent jobs, I suppose. The hours fit my life well. We are getting by alright. Life is that way. You know, I can hardly believe Crissy is almost four. Time goes by too fast."

The conversation goes on for a while, then Avery switches it up as the server collected our plates and refilled our lemonades.

"You know Patty, we have been friends for a long time. Well, I just thought I would kinda... maybe... say... that you might want to leave the trucking jobs to the boys. You know, maybe... think about going back to nursing school? You know your mom really wanted that for you."

Beautiful Avery, with her auburn hair curled around her shoulders, is nervously tapping her glass, and she put me on the spot. I pause a minute before answering.

"I know you see my mom often, and I appreciate that. Mom always considered you a daughter, too. I never wanted to disappoint my family and friends, and it feels very much like I have let everyone down. Nobody understands that this is the happiest I have ever been. I just saw Mom, and she is trying to come to terms with it."

"But it just seems so wrong, Patty. It's like you are running away or something."

I looked straight at my friend. "It's hard to explain the gut feeling when you aren't fitting in, and you aren't happy. That feeling that comes with deciding what would be best as a career. I am just saying that the job I am doing makes me happy, what makes my gears mesh, so to speak. Bottom line is that I am in a career that I absolutely love. It's a different kind of challenge."

"I don't understand," Avery said, with her head down.

"I don't expect anyone ever will." I smiled and assured my friend that sometimes we are cut from a different cloth. We said our goodbyes and promised not to wait so long to meet again. Avery's words rattled in my head that entire evening and I was trying not to doubt myself, even though I knew this was the right direction for my life.

I shook off Avery's discouragement. Sleep finally came, but it was a short night. My feet hit the floor at about 2:30 am. Both Mark and I were at the shop on time.

We say little to each other, and Larry is busy on the phone with a driver who broke down somewhere and he isn't at the window to say hello. Our paperwork was in our boxes. I took a moment to ask Mark a question as we were gathering up our bills of lading and run sheets for our loads.

"When we stop en route, can I take a minute and call the customer for directions?"

"I have you covered for this load, Patty," Mark said as he was filling out a few lines to begin his run sheet. "Stop worrying and just let me get you there."

"Okay, sorry. One more question, Mark, if you don't mind?"

He barely glanced up as I spoke.

"Can you be polite and drop all the sexual comments, please?"

"No promises."

We found our reefer trailers dropped right next to each other, and we got hooked up without issue. We both checked our load temps to make sure the setting was minus ten degrees and set on a continuous run.

This temp won't freeze the meat because of how densely it's packed in the cases. Minus ten degrees will keep the meat ice cold and fresh until delivery. I didn't ask Mark about his reefer fuel level, mine was full. The two drivers who ran these loads together would have probably fueled at the same time. Our trucks are all packed and pre-trips done; we are pulling out of the terminal at exactly 4 am.

I reached up into the little cubbyhole above my head and turned on my new CB radio. Carlos was kind enough to put it in for me. We will communicate on some level, but I am unsure what conversations we are going to have.

To my surprise, Mark hardly said a word for the first few hours. By 9 am we are near Lodi, Ohio. My stomach is growling.

"Hey Mark," I said over the CB, "How about we stop at Lodi and get some breakfast?"

"Yes, that sounds good," came back across my speakers and I recognized Mark's voice. The CB radio is public, so everything being said can be heard by others who may be tuned in. Sometimes a stray comment will come across from a stranger, but none did.

We both parked, and then went inside for breakfast.

I had my clipboard with me so I could organize my paperwork, start my run sheet, and hopefully get directions while sitting still at a table. We sat down and ordered our food. Without warning, Mark started talking nonsense.

"So, Patty, why are you here? Why are you driving a truck? Can't you find enough dick at home?" He said all that without taking a breath.

"What? Why are you asking me that stuff? I live an hour away from the shop and if I wanted a man, I would have one. Right now, I am trying to focus on getting my career off the ground."

The server took our breakfast orders and brought coffee to our table.

Mark wasn't done with me yet. "You are taking a man's job and it's not right."

After hearing that I needed to tread carefully, Mark was a time bomb, so I spoke carefully. "Do you know someone who is out of work?"

"Yea, my brother-in-law and I can't get him out of my house." Hate poured out of Mark's mouth.

"Listen Mark, what work has he done in the past? What is he qualified to do? Can he drive?" I asked, cautiously.

"No, he isn't qualified to drive a truck. His last job was construction, and he's a good roofer."

"Well then, I am not taking a job from your brother-in-law. Besides, the trucking industry has a shortage of drivers, so if he wants to learn, I am sure someone could train him."

Total silence from Mark while I was sorting through my paperwork, searching for directions. A while back, I overheard a couple of drivers talk about directions to the customers. They are supposed to be printed somewhere in the stack of paperwork.

Mark sat across from me, looking peeved.

"Women do a lot of jobs you might not agree with."

"Like what?" Mark asked, coldly.

"Well, there are women engineers, professors, doctors, lawyers, pilots, welders, women in the military. Would you like me to go on? It's a long list."

"Shut up, stupid, and let me eat."

"No way, Mark, you brought this up and I am not done yet. What about men who do jobs you may think of as feminine?"

Mark looked up like I just spoke a foreign language, and he couldn't leave that one alone. "Men are men and women are women, and you belong at home barefoot and pregnant."

'Screw you, Mark' came to mind, but I didn't say that aloud.

"What about male nurses? What about men who raise their kids? What about men who are traveling salesmen and sleep in hotels? Women do that line of work too, and it doesn't mean they are out looking for dick, as you call it. Both men and women are teachers, clerks, cashiers, short-order cooks, fancy chefs, CEOs with respectable companies and the list goes on."

"Okay, fine, you made your point, but it's still not right that you are driving a truck."

"Can I call ahead for directions before we leave?"

"No, and let's go. We're wasting time."

I left the tip next to my coffee cup unnoticed by my not-so-happy babysitter.

It was a wintry day; a few inches of snow had recently fallen and left the highway a little greasy in spots. We had freezing rain about half-way across, which formed long icicles on the bottom of the mirrors and iced up everything. We had to slow down and be careful through that snowy mess. The weather front moved out once we passed the east side of Snowshoe Mountain in Pennsylvania. Dad was right. Freezing cold air went right past my driver's door seal and froze my left leg.

I pulled my coat over my lap, and that helped. Trucks most definitely do rattle, groan, and freeze us. Interstate 80 through Pennsylvania was in very poor condition. The potholes were huge, and the concrete was busted up so badly in spots that we needed to use the left lane often. The hills were a learning curve, too.

We geared down to climb up the grades and the rule of thumb is to go down the hill in the same low gear as you climbed up. Sometimes, however, the engine will bog down too much. We needed to up-shift, coming down the other side. Depending on how steep the grade is, there can be a lot of danger if a driver isn't paying attention and goes down a hill too fast with a loaded trailer. The hotter brakes get, the less effective they become and can cause a truck to get out of control in a quick hurry and crash. This dilemma led to the creation of emergency truck escape ramps being placed at regular intervals along the downhill sections of mountains throughout the United States. These escape ramps have saved many lives. With that said, our brakes were warm a few times because our trucks didn't have a compression system or jake brake as it's called to control our truck speed. We kept our speed in moderation, and it all went fine.

It took us a few more hours traveling through Pennsylvania before we stopped one last time for fuel. This truck stop was called Buckhorn, and it had a hunter's lodge feel. There was a fireplace in the dining room. Eating there would have been a great experience but will have to wait for a future time. I was starving and got a sandwich, coffee, and a couple of donuts to go. Mark didn't want to eat. We fueled and knocked any remaining ice off of our trucks. We continued on our way.

It was late afternoon, and we were ahead of schedule. The sun was setting, glinting brightly in my eyes from the side mirrors. Traffic was steady and we're caught up in New Jersey post rush hour traffic, heavy in spots. Finally, about two hours after leaving the Buckhorn truck stop, there were signs for Paterson. We were going past the exits to the city, and I knew something wasn't right.

Mark chimed up over the CB radio, "Take the next exit and follow the ramp to the right then turn right again at the first light. Go two blocks and your customer is at the end of the street. After you get unloaded, don't forget about getting the trailer washed out."

"Okay, thanks," I remembered Mark saying in one of our brief conversations that fresh meat leaks through the boxes and leaves blood on the trailer floor. The trailer wash company wasn't too far from Paterson, and the directions for the wash were on my paperwork. There were no directions for the customer and Mark refused to let me make that call. I was instructed to trust him. I absolutely knew I couldn't.

My exit came up fast, and the traffic was heavy. I took the exit Mark insisted on and followed the exit ramp to the right. It's a sweeping ramp with no way to get back onto the highway. I turned right at the next light and immediately got a sick feeling in the pit of my stomach. It only took a moment for me to realize this was not an exit for any business other than a couple of bars, a strip club, and a gas station.

This was an old historic neighborhood with narrow streets. Of course, Mark and Brian had set me up. How on earth am I going to safely turn this truck around and get out of here? The street Mark sent me down was a residential neighborhood full of post-war houses built tightly together.

As I eased the truck down the first block, it was clear that I couldn't make a left or right turn on the side street because the streets were far too narrow. I know I am in trouble. Cars were parked on both sides of the street, making the situation worse. It looked like a dead-end up ahead, just past the second block.

My other option was to back the rig up to find another street that would be big enough to handle my truck. This wouldn't be possible, however, with impatient drivers all around, and center point steering makes a loaded truck hard to maneuver. I continued on and saw the second block was just as narrow as the first, but with little choice left, I went down it anyway, hoping it didn't dead-end. I was so close to the cars on both sides that it made me tense and worried about scraping a car door.

About half-way down the second block, I stopped and put my 4-way flashers on. I walked down to the end of the street, and to my great relief, I saw it wasn't a dead end after all. The street turned left at the end, and it looked wide enough.

I felt confident that if I took that left turn, I could find my way back to the highway and locate a phone to call the customer for directions. My spirits lifted tremendously when I saw an out with only one obstacle preventing me from making that left turn, a car parked so close to the corner that I couldn't clear it while making that left turn.

Who owns that car? Are they home? A lot of thoughts went through my head as I tried to guess which house belonged to the car owner.

My heart raced as I walked up to the door, hoping that it might be the right house. I stepped onto a well-manicured porch and knocked on the door twice and to my great relief, someone was home.

"Whatdayawant?" I was facing a man in the doorway holding a beer, wearing plaid undershorts and nothing else.

"Bbbbrrraaapppp," was the next thing he uttered after he took a long chug from his can.

I stood there smiling big with my hands clenched behind my back, feeling ridiculous.

"A not-so-helpful driver sent me down the wrong exit. I can almost get off this street, but that car sitting on the corner is in my way."

"You don't by any chance own that car, do you?" I was smiling, and he wasn't.

"Yea, that's my car alright, what's it worth to ya to have me move it?" Okay, he wants to negotiate. There is hope.

"How about $20 bucks?" I asked with a big stupid smile.

"It's a deal for $50 bucks, bbbbrrraaapppp."

"How about $35?"

He looked over at my truck, paused a long moment, and assessed that I could not make the corner without his help.

"I will take $40 bucks and pay attention to where you are going next time. But hey girlie, it's your lucky day 'cause you look like my little niece, so I will help you."

"My money is in the truck, so give me a second." I ran to the truck, and he disappeared from the doorway to put some clothes on. I hoped anyway.

I ran back up onto his porch. He re-appeared with pants, shoes, and no shirt, which surprised me. It was cold outside. The man grabbed the money out of my hand, then he stepped off the porch to hold up his end of the bargain. I thanked him.

After making that turn, the road swung around to a stoplight. Straight ahead, just a short distance, was the ramp to the highway and the same gas station. I parked along the curb and went inside the gas station with a question and an address.

"Excuse me, does anyone know where I might find this place?"

Two men walked over to me, looked at my paperwork, and neither of them knew where this place was.

The clerk spoke up, "Come over here and I will let you use my phone to call an operator. She might be able to locate the number."

The operator quickly found the number. I wrote it down on the back of my hand and asked the clerk if I could make the call for directions.

"You certainly can, happy to help you, ma'am."

The customer answered right away, and I explained where I was according to the exit number.

"You are close, just head back west two exits, follow the ramp straight, then make a left at the second light. We will unload you as soon as you get here. Back into door five and check in after that with your paperwork and rear seal. We need your load."

Fifteen minutes later, I was backing in. As soon as I bumped the dock and set my brakes, I felt and heard a loud clonk as a worker dropped the dock plate into the trailer. They were eager to unload me. We shared some small talk about how good their business was doing. In no time at all, I was empty and heading to the trailer wash. That ordeal confirmed the deliberate trick that Mark and Brian came up with to drop me off in the middle of a busy residential area with the hope it would be career-ending. It was nowhere near career-ending and I got through this unscathed. Only forty bucks lighter, and I learned a valuable lesson about trust and trip planning. Trust was the big lesson of the day.

Finding the trailer wash was easy. "How much will this cost?" I asked the guy at the desk, trying to figure out in my head how much money I would need. I only had $60.00 left in my pocket.

"No charge missy, your company has an account here."

"That's great. Can I sleep here?" I asked, knowing that finding a place to sleep this late at night would be impossible.

"Sure, just park in back and nobody will bother you."

Sleep came fast. I was exhausted, and nobody bothered me, just as the man had promised.

My alarm jangled at 6 am. I got dressed and opened my curtains to welcome a new day. Nothing was near my truck except for a few dropped trailers. I needed a restroom and a phone. After getting dressed, I walked up to the main building and explained that they had washed my trailer out last night.

The clerk was a different guy and just as friendly.

"May I use your restroom and phone?" I asked politely, and he was perfectly fine with both requests.

"Yes ma'am, and we have a shower in the ladies' room if you want to take advantage of that."

"Yes, absolutely, thank you."

I walked back out to my truck to grab my bags and a fresh set of clothes. I must have looked awful with my hair all tangled from sleeping all night. It was so nice to get a shower on site.

~ ~

Chapter Four

Brian Isn't Giving Up & Lot Lizards

Before calling Brian, I had thought about this prank at length and knew there were lots of ways to handle this. My decision in the end was to take the high road and act as though Mark got me exactly to the customer like they had never tricked me.

My best guess was that Mark didn't know where the meat market was. I was going to ride that assumption, knowing Brian played a role as well.

"Good morning, Brian," I said when he picked up on the first ring.

"What's good about it?" He answered, sounding like a bear.

"It's a beautiful Friday. Where am I picking up the backhaul? The trailer is empty and washed out. I am ready to go."

Long pause over the phone, "Ummmm... how did you do with Mark? Did he get you there all right?"

I answered chipper, "It went perfect, he got me right to their door."

"He did WHAT!? Ooohhhh, I mean that's good Patty." After a long pause and a sigh in my ear, Brian dispatched me.

"I am sending you to Lewistown, PA, to pick up a load of paper going to Birmingham, Alabama. Delivery is Monday at 8 am central time. The load picks up at 1 pm this afternoon. It's an 800-mile run from Lewistown, PA. You have 220 miles of deadhead to get your load. After you unload the paper in Birmingham, stay put. The next morning, you are picking up a load of frozen potatoes. That backhaul isn't too far away from where you will be. As soon as you unload the paper on Monday, you will need to pre-cool your reefer unit to minus twenty degrees. That load comes to the yard. Can you handle it?"

"Yes, but I am really short on money."

"No problem, I can put money on your fuel card. Will a hundred bucks see you through?"

"Yes, thank you."

We have the liberty of pulling cash advances from our paychecks if we need it. I will pick up the cash at my next fuel stop.

Brian gave me the load number, name, and address of both customers. I arrived at the paper mill right on schedule, loaded, and out of there by 3 pm. This will be an easy two-day drive.

After driving all day, I stopped for the night at a little mom-and-pop truck stop near Knoxville, Tennessee. A pretty server with her hair tied back was delighted to take my order. She brought me a cup of coffee and then she asked if I would like the special. "The ham steaks are delicious," she said enthusiastically.

"Yes, that would be great, thank you."

A few minutes later, she brought me a large ham steak with red-eye gravy, a big scoop of mashed potatoes, a steaming pile of vegetables, and two fresh pieces of cornbread with tons of butter. I could barely eat it all. She was my first encounter with southern hospitality. She smiled, set down the check, then shocked me with her comment, "I give good service to everyone, even though the ladies don't tip."

I left her a large tip and wrote on the napkin: "Women aren't all equal. I always tip, and you deserved it. Nice job."

So far, I have had no truck stop issues other than Eunice with the giant dice earrings. This is about to change is a big way at my next break.

Birmingham was a busy place, and I was delivering to a company east of the city. I saw several trucks lined up, waiting their turn. I got out of the truck and went inside to find the receiving office.

"It's going to be several hours before your turn. We are running behind today. Just wait in your truck and someone will be out to get you when it's time." The lady said from the other side of the receiving window. I walked back to my truck. It felt warm outside, like a spring morning, a far cry from Indiana, which was still winter. The sky was a beautiful blue with big puffy clouds.

A couple of curious drivers walked over to chat with me. These guys introduced themselves as west-coast drivers. We chatted quite a while outside of our trucks.

One of them had a 1979 Kenworth W900 with a big cam 400 Cummins engine and a 13-speed transmission. He even had a jake brake, impressive. The other driver had a big, beautiful Peterbilt with lots of shiny chrome, along with all the bells and whistles.

"Yea, this girl will do about 110 on through the desert." The Kenworth guy said with a grin. "The smokey bears leave us big rigs alone. I won't go east of Ohio; too much traffic and hassle."

We talked about the wide-open spaces and the big sky of the west. We talked about stuff like highway construction, bridges, rivers, valleys, mountains, and the beautiful wide-open spaces.

"You haven't lived until you see a western sunset. The beauty of the sky will overwhelm you with the pinks, purples and reds going across the horizon."

"I have seen some gorgeous purple and red sunsets in the Midwest," I said, trying to sound relevant. They go on about this and that and when the talk changed to checking out their upholstery. Male drivers frequently asked that question during conversations. Guys aren't bad, some are just opportunistic.

"No thanks, I will pass." I turned away and got into my truck. After a bit, I crawled into my bunk and fell asleep. Several hours into my nap, I got the knock on the door to unload. The West Coast guys were long gone by then.

Later that evening, I made it to a large truck stop in Birmingham. The place was packed, and I drove around for a few minutes trying to find a parking spot. Luckily, I found one in the back row. Little did I know this truck stop was a central point for every lot lizard in the entire state of Alabama. Or at least it seemed that way.

After I parked, I watched in disbelief as women walked from truck to truck, knocking on doors. I needed to go inside to use the restroom and maybe catch a late supper. I don't know how I will do that without being grabbed, arrested, harassed, or assaulted.

Even my door gets a knock. "No thanks," I told her, and she just smiled at me and said, "I do either men or women. I can do you honey; money is money."

"I will pass," I said, feeling totally creeped out. She knocked on several more truck doors before a driver further down the row let her in. Often, the lot lizards will knock on truck doors to ask the drivers if they can just sit in their trucks and use their CB radios to drum up business. I was asked that question too. "Miss driver, may I sit in your truck and use your radio?"

"No, my radio is broken." It wasn't broken, but I wasn't having any of those women in my truck. I had already shut it off because of the squawking noise of truckers talking over each other and hollering for the lizards, or just hollering for no reason. Some truckers use the CB radio just to argue and stir up trouble. My fib worked, and she left me alone.

After a half-hour of watching all this happening, I badly needed to go inside, so I stepped out of my truck, locked my doors, and started walking across the lot. The air smelled strongly of urine. Men pee next to their trucks, creating an awful stench that wafts up from the asphalt. As I made my way through the parked trucks heading up to the main building, I saw drivers flashing their headlights and blasting their horns to signal for women. One driver hollered out his window, straight at me.

"Hey wench, how 'bout a blowjob?" I tucked my arms tight around myself as I walked past his truck, ignoring him.

He gets mad and screams, "Hey, you wench, get back here! I said I wanted a blowjob!"

I walked faster, still ignoring him. This place looked like a rock concert with the truck headlights flashing for women. This truck stop was crawling with lot lizards, and I felt terribly unsafe walking through the rows of parked trucks.

I walked a little faster and then realized I was being followed. My gut felt alarmed, and then a moment later, a man firmly grabbed my arm. I quickly pulled out my switchblade and met him with a sharp edge.

"Hey whoa driver," said a stranger, "I am parked right next to you, and I thought I would walk with you to go inside."

I stopped on a dime and turned to look at him. "Seriously? You scared the life out of me just to help?"

"Sorry I scared you, but you are a girl walking alone. I didn't want you to have a problem. I am a family man and part-time farmer at home."

"You scared the life out of me and yes, I probably could use your help. Sorry I pulled my blade on you."

"You're forgiven." The stranger stuck his hand out. "My name is Curt."

"Hi Curt, I'm Patty." We ate a midnight supper together. I listened over vegetable soup and a grilled ham and cheese sandwich as he talked about his wife and kids, trying to balance his life around his jobs. Curt sounded like he needed a friend more than I did. It made me happy to have a man nearby who wasn't trying to get a piece. After we ate and talked for a while, we walked safely back to our trucks.

"Lock your door," he said, like a concerned friend. He waited for me to press down my door lock, and then he climbed up in his own truck, locked it up, and closed his curtains.

He was a brief friend who filled a need that I had for my safety while walking through a dangerous parking lot on a winter night in Birmingham. I know he felt safer too.

I haven't closed my curtains yet because I am watching a lizard climbing out of a truck in the row in front of me. There is nothing too remarkable about that, considering where I am for the night. It seemed odd that she was holding up her pants up. With mild curiosity, I watched her as she walked past my truck and then she stopped directly beside my trailer tandems. She squats down low and pees. She never looked up to see if anyone was watching her, and it was highly doubtful that she would even care. That did it for me and I closed my curtains.

There must be a better way to make a living. All this lies somewhere far beyond my comprehension. Three guesses as to what happens to a driver trying to sleep in a lizard-infested truck stop. Knock... knock... knock every few minutes that reached well into the night.

The women had no care in the least that you need to sleep. They are persistent as hell until the cops round them up, or they just pack up and leave on their own.

My morning started with a shower. I had to pay the woman at the counter ten bucks for a shower key and a ratty towel, which I laid on the floor in front of the sink. I packed my own towels from home. The door opened up to a small room crammed with a shower stall, toilet, and sink. The room smelled funky. Truck stop showers are a crapshoot. Sometimes you might have hot water, or more likely room temperature water, because it costs too much to heat it. Some truck stop showers have plastic curtains that have layers of mold or just yuck that you don't want to know about. I figured out early that flip-flops or beach sandals are a must for protecting my feet. Dad always had a raging athlete's foot itch. Of course, it was from public showers.

Much better showers with actual hot water and many refurbishments were years away. It took the industry a long time to figure out that a nice shower makes a happy customer, and a happy customer will spend money at your store.

After that, I ordered a breakfast of bacon, eggs, and over-buttered toast swimming on a plate of grease, all served up by a friendly woman who remembered to refill my coffee cup. Full cup equals tip, simple.

Before pulling out, I set my reefer to minus twenty and topped off my truck and reefer fuel. I made it over to the frozen food company right on time. There were trucks already waiting, but they got me loaded within two hours. I called Brian, and he told me to drive straight back.

"It's about 700 miles to the yard from where you loaded. Be here tonight."

"Okay, no problem." Trucking companies disregarded logbooks in this era. We were part of the equipment and nothing else.

The drive back north on I-65 was good. It was a gorgeous sunny day. The landscape was green and lush, and the highway was smooth. There was the occasional billboard for Stuckey's, offering Two eggs, toast & jelly for 99 cents.

The CB radio was alive with chatter, which I successfully ignored for a while until my radio picked up a conversation between two drivers that were talking about a server that one of them decided he was in love with. Everybody within earshot listened and stayed quiet.

"Hey, Bubba, whatdya mean she ain't in love with me! You shoulda seen how big her smile was. I remember she had killer curves too, and those beautiful legs went all the way to heaven. That girl is mine. I just gotta go get her."

"Lookie here, Tator, she was only after a big tip. They all want big tips; stop sounding like a dumb hick."

"Well, I surely got somethin big for my sweetie!"

"The only thing you got that's big, Tator, is your pie hole."

"Well, that ain't nice Bubba."

"My honey waits tables up here just a few miles at the Nashville Union 76 and I just know she's a waitin on me to come back. In fact, I might just scoop her up and toss that sweet thing into my truck and haul her off."

"That's kidnapping Tator, and just how long ago did she wait on you? Do even remember her name?"

"Ahhh, I dunno maybe four months ago, but I remember that smile and I'm a gonna claim her as soon as I get stopped up here. I'm a thinkin her name was Darla, or somethin like that."

"So, let me get this straight Tator, you are going to stop up here at the Union 76, get fuel and get parked, then you are going into the restaurant to scoop up a server? You aren't even sure what her name is? You're kidding me, right?"

"So, Bubba, you gonna stop up here with me?"

"I really need to get myself down the road. I might catch up with you sometime."

"Now you know that's a bad excuse, and we've been runnin down this highway together for hours now. Come on now, you gotta meet my sweetie pie."

"Okay, fine, Tator, I am kinda hungry anyway. We are going to order lunch and that's it. Please don't get us arrested. I aint going to jail cause of you."

Three trucks exited the highway behind me. No doubt we were all curious about Tator's honey, and assuming it's all coming from an old memory, this could be great fun.

Bubba and Tator were talking about mile markers. They were coming up from behind.

My fuel was okay, so I parked and then set the reefer on defrost. Reefers can ice up and quit running if a driver doesn't do a manual defrost every so often. They aren't advanced units yet. I walked inside the building and heard Faron Young singing Hello Walls, followed by Hank Snow singing Movin' On. Truck stops play this stuff around the clock. The bathrooms were clean. I washed up, then walked into the half-full restaurant. The three drivers who walked in moments ahead of me invited me to sit with them. I was happy to join them, and we introduced ourselves around the table.

No sign of Bubba or Tator yet. Cigarette smoke hung heavy, and the clang of dishes and nearby conversations filled the room. A server in her 50s introduced herself as Miss Elly. She had a young trainee following behind who looked brand new.

"Hello, I am Penny," she said in a soft voice, as she placed the water glasses with Miss Elly's approval. She took our orders, which amounted to burgers and fries, then she trotted off to the kitchen. We didn't have to wait long. Here comes Bubba and Tator. We knew it was them by the shit-eating grin on the first guy, like he owned the joint. He was smoothing his shiny Bryl-creamed hair and checking out the dining room for the perfect table. The second guy looked like he just bit into a lemon. They found a table about half-way between us and the kitchen. We had a great view.

Tator starts right in just a shoutin and a hollerin, "Where are you Darla, you sweet thing? Papa is here and I know you remember me. Come on out, honey!"

"Shut up, Tator, you're gonna get us arrested or thrown out."

Miss Elly comes out of the kitchen to see what the fuss was about.

"Where's my woman!" Tator demands.

"Excuse me, sir, I am not having this ruckus in my restaurant. The only women working here are me and a new trainee and you've already scared her half to death. Put a lid on it and I am not warning you twice. Do you understand me?"

The four of us were smirking, giggling, and taking bets on how long it took Bubba to run out the door and Tator to get hauled off. Bubba was sitting there rubbing his face and looking extremely embarrassed. Miss Elly reluctantly took their orders.

"I should've had the good sense to throw you both out, so order right this second or leave." Miss Elly shouted, looking like a storm cloud.

They immediately ordered whatever the special was. Some chicken dish, of course, made from leftovers. Within a minute or two, Penny comes out of the kitchen with a tray of food.

She steered clear of their table to serve customers. But when she returned to the kitchen, she got sidetracked and unfortunately walked close to Tator. His face broke into a wide grin and his arm shot out. He grabbed himself a big chunk of her ass cheek. Penny screamed, dropped the tray, and slapped Tator hard right across his face. He grabbed the back of her dress and yanked her onto his lap. Her pretty robin egg blue dress flew up. Penny screamed for help and screamed some more. Bubba ran out the door right that second. Fast as lightning. Gone!

All four of us and a couple more guys immediately jumped up to pull Penny off Tator's lap and get her upright. She ran into the kitchen, nearly knocking Miss Elly over as she came bombing out of the kitchen, holding a full pot of scalding hot coffee.

Miss Elly was yelling at the top of her lungs, "The police are on their way! How DARE you assault Penny, HOW DARE YOU!" Miss Elly could've woken the dead right then.

Miss Elly lost her temper and cracked the coffee pot hard against Tator's head. 'KA-WHAMMM! The pot shattered and thrust hot coffee and glass all over him, the table, and the floor. Tator hollered and jumped up, causing his chair to tip over. Tator fell flat on the floor, directly into the glass and into the mess. He slowly picked himself up, his chair up, and then he picked glass shards out of his greased hair and ear. He sat back down, stunned. Bright red patches were on appearing on his face and neck from being scalded.

A guy at a nearby table calmly walked over and handed Tator a stack of napkins to sop up the blood running down his temple. He leaned over the table, maybe three inches from Tator's face. "You're a dumbass," he said. Then he calmly walked back to his table and gracefully sat down, smooth as silk. That scene could have been straight from a Sam Elliott movie. The entire restaurant was clapping and hooting. We are all on our feet cheering miss Elly and offering our help.

A maintenance man came to the rescue with a mop and bucket, and everything was quickly settled when the police arrived. Two officers read Tator his rights. He was cuffed, taken outside, and the officers stuffed him into the squad car. We were all entertained watching this unfold from the big glass windows.

Penny served our food and thanked us for helping her. We had a great time chatting, eating, and laughing together. We all agreed that was the best show in a long time and definitely worth a stop.

Most of the trip back was stormy. I drove north to Indiana with temperature changes from warm to cool to cold. A couple of intense thunderstorms with spectacular lightning gave me an outstanding storm-sky show coming up through Kentucky. The hard rain and wind sheers reminded me how powerful mother nature can be. Cars were driving slowly with their 4-ways on just trying to navigate the highways in the heavy downpours. There are tremendous visual advantages of sitting up higher in a truck. It was after midnight when I made my last stop for fuel and a snack coming up through Indiana.

The yard was finally in sight. It's 3 am and pitch dark. I geared down into 2nd, easing the rig into the lot, then drove to the back. I dropped the trailer on the loaded pad. Sleep is on my agenda as soon as I get home. That long drive took a toll on me. I made the mistake of walking inside. Larry saw me.

"Hi Patty, I have your next dispatch." Larry handed me a wad of paperwork.

"What is it?" I asked, not wanting to go anywhere but home.

"It's a hot load of auto parts sitting in the yard going to Rockford, Illinois and orders from Brian that you deliver it asap." I was told to leave out right then, and I explained to Larry that I was beyond tired from driving straight back from Alabama, per orders.

Patty, there's a message from Brian that if you don't accept dispatch, you'll be fired.

"Of course, Brian did this."

I had no choice but to try somehow to wake up and take that load to Rockford, Illinois. The trailer was sitting out back, close to the load I had just sat down. This run will be brutally hard.

I drove those four and a half hours with my head out the window at times and stopping a few times to run laps around the truck. The fresh air can help wake up a driver along with about a half-gallon of coffee, but it didn't help me much that trip.

I traveled west along the Indiana toll road, then through Chicago. There were a few service plazas along the way, but I couldn't take too much extra time.

Thanks to my guardian angel, I reached Rockford by 7 am central time. I was blurry eyed, tired, and my body hurt from fatigue. The receiver unloaded the truck quickly, even though he said this load wasn't due until next week. He didn't understand the rush to deliver.

Of course, it wasn't supposed to be delivered early; I thought to myself. Brian can't admit defeat.

Just before leaving, I asked the receiver if I could park on the property and sleep for a little while and he tells me that's not a problem. I parked outside of the guard shack in a perimeter gravel lot. In fact, it was many acres of a large vacant lot. Sound sleep came instantly, and I didn't stir until 6 pm. I woke up with a start, sitting bolt upright in my bunk, not remembering where I was or why I was there. What day is this? Wednesday?

It's Wednesday evening. I slept soundly for ten hours! It took a few moments for the fuzz to clear from my head and my thoughts put back together. The sun was setting and everything looked different. The huge gravel lot was barren except for my truck.

The giant auto factory was in the distance. I remember the events; I remember unloading and then asking the receiver if I could sleep.

My bladder was the next thing on my mind as I dressed. I found a clean shirt, combed my hair, and slid my jeans on. There were no bathrooms clear out here in the middle of nowhere, and no way would I go back inside the gate. That's never allowed. Once a driver's job was done at any location, you're out of there after passing through the exit gate. I got out to stretch, then peed next to my fuel tank, something similar to a cow in a flat rock. I tossed my used paper towel into my trash bag.

I rolled out after getting my bearings and soon found a truck stop nearby and I pulled in. It was evening, and the place was deserted. I decided to just park on the fuel island for five minutes to wash my hands and face. The clerk had just made coffee, so I bought a large cup and a tuna sandwich from the deli case. Those can give you food poisoning, but I was starving and took the risk. Sometimes it's better not to think about it.

I didn't go into the office when I got back. I stuffed the signed bills into an after-hours paperwork box and went home. This is what Ron meant when he said, "Make the company look good." A reference to logbooks. Translation - we will run you to death and you can't do anything about it. Home was a welcome sight. Surprisingly, my phone didn't ring.

I got my clothes washed, picked up my mail from my kind neighbor, then stopped past the bank to deposit my paycheck. The following morning, I went to work intending to talk to Ron.

I wasn't under a load yet, but I packed my bags just in case. I parked my car and walked into the building, relieved to see no sign of Bill, Mark, or Roger, who continue to give me problems. They won't let up and Harold warned me about saying even one word about it. Harold's obnoxious behavior makes all of this even worse.

The driver's room was still just as dirty as ever and for the first time, I noticed a payphone in the corner and wondered why I had never noticed it before.

Within a minute, Ron comes out of his office.

"Good morning, Ron. I need to talk to you."

"Morning Patty, come in and have a seat. What brings you in to see me?"

"It's about the abusive treatment from Brian. Things have been going great. Then I get back from a several-hundred-mile stretch just to learn that I must take a hot load to Rockford, IL asap. That auto plant had tons of those parts, and the receiver said I was a week early. So, what's this all about?"

"Well, for starters, Brian is the best dispatcher this company has ever seen."

"You can't run a trucking company with dead drivers," I said.

"I don't see a problem. Maybe you slackers should step up."

"I understand now what you were telling us about doing our logs to make the company look good. We are required to lie and cheat our logs just to squeeze in more runs."

"This is how companies maintain profits." Ron said, unapologetically.

"That's illegal and dangerous, Ron."

We all became distracted when Lisa walked into Ron's office with some paperwork and Harold was two steps behind her, sniffing her hair. "Knock it off, Harold!" Ron said, annoyed.

"I can do as I please." Harold said, smugly.

There was nothing more to say to Ron. I walked outside and there was Steve, the same Steve who recommended this job to me.

"Hey Patty, how is it going? I have been so busy it's hard to keep up with everyone."

"I am ok Steve, it's good to see you. Ron and I just went around about being run half to death."

We both walked outside because Brian monitors what's being said in the driver area.

"What happened?" Steve asked.

"I slept ten hours in Rockford before heading back to the yard." I stopped short of saying much else. It wasn't Steve's problem, and I didn't want to sound like I was whining. Steve only nodded and looked down without commenting.

"Another issue I have, Steve, is that I can't get away from the rude comments from a few other drivers."

"Your best defense is to just laugh, and they will give up."

"I have been doing that. I can't figure out Bill. He wants to date me, and he is so pushy. He's asked me out at least five times and I'm not interested. And why does he smell so bad?"

"Bill has been living is his truck. I guess he can't smell himself. Everyone has been gagging around him lately. Anyway, Bill has a young son with Cerebral Palsy, and he blames his wife, and from what I hear, she doesn't have much to do with him. He puts the entire burden on her, which isn't fair. I am certain that she only stays married for the financial support and honestly, not sure how long she will even do that."

"Well, the court would make him pay child support." I said.

"Yes, which is why he is still with her. He has talked to me about it and the court ordered support would far exceed the measly amount he gives her now."

After hearing that, my opinion of Bill was below pond scum, and I wanted nothing to do with him.

~ ~

Chapter Five

Dealing with Mark & A Date with Zachary

Time passed, winter became spring, and the work is ongoing. The log issues will never be resolved. We are expected to drive until we drop, and those were the rules, period. We were often tired, but the bills didn't stop. Some drivers are mortgaged to the hilt and must take the abuse or starve to death and lose everything. Trucking companies notoriously hold this over our heads. It takes thousands of fatigue crashes before the industry makes it illegal to run drivers half to death. Trucking in the 1980s was decades away from making safety a priority in the trucking industry. Fortunately, these changes eventually happen, and safety becomes front and center.

It's a beautiful Monday in April, and I just pulled in from a weekend run. My truck was due for service, so I know I will at least have the rest of the day off. Bill, Mark, and Roger were still up to no good. Leroy stopped hanging with them a while back because he was so embarrassed by their behavior. We have all seen Leroy hanging out with Carlos, which is great.

I walked into the driver's room and, of course, Bill and Roger were sitting at a table. They start right in again and I am trying to distance myself from these guys the best I can. There was a horrible body odor wafting up from Bill, gagging everybody.

"Don't you guys ever go to work?" I asked, and of course they ignored that question.

"Hey Patty, do you live on a chicken farm? Because you sure know how to raise a cock." Roger said, howling.

"Hey Patty, do you know the difference between my dick and a chicken wing? Let's go find out. How about Sunday?" Bill said.

"Can you guys please stop this? I am not interested, and you know that. I have worked here for over six months. Please stop harassing me!"

They both completely ignored me and looked me up and down like I was prey.

Mark walked into the driver's room right after I made my plea. He shocked everyone by going in an entirely different direction with the conversation.

"Hey Patty, I owe you an apology for being a jerk on that run we did together a while back. How about letting me take you to breakfast?"

"Well, that's a surprise, and that happened months ago. No thanks, I am not ready to trust you yet. It's going to take a while longer, if ever."

Everyone jumped in on that idea. Even creepy Harold was walking through and heard Mark offer me breakfast. Lisa briefly distracted Harold when she handed Brian a stack of paperwork. He chased after her to look down at her cleavage. She shot him a dirty look. Harold instantly got back on track and offered his two cents.

"Oh, for crying out loud Patty, just go with Mark and let him apologize."

"Why should I trust his offer for an apology, Harold? He probably wants to dump my body somewhere. This stinks to high Heaven."

"Good grief, just go," Harold said, exasperated.

"If I agree, where would we go?"

"A little place just down the road, maybe twenty minutes. They have great food."

"Okay, I guess so." I absolutely didn't want to go.

Mark ran out the door and, in a flash, he pulled up gunning the engine of a 1970 something beat up Chevy pickup. It needed a muffler.

"Hang on a second. I need to go to my truck to check something."

"Check what?"

"Nothing much. I will be right back."

My key slid easily into the door lock. I quickly climbed into the cab and found my little canister of pepper spray. The pepper spray fit easily into the right pocket of my jeans, and I slid my switchblade into the left pocket. I climbed out of my truck and locked it.

Someone was behind me. I caught a whiff of Bill, but before I could step away, he pinned me against my truck and started to hump my ass.

"Get off me, you stinky sonofabitch! You smell like a garbage can." The wind was up drafting his stink right into my nose. I dug my elbow firmly into his ribs and, with all my strength, gave him a forceful shove. He lost his balance and fell to the ground, hard. He slowly got back up, holding his side, wincing.

"That hurt! I think you cracked a rib."

"I hope so. You deserved that. I was hoping to crack your head, too." I said, pleased with myself.

Bill took two steps towards me. He was filthy from head to toe and his hair was greasy and matted. He was a walking dumpster.

"Gimme your phone number."

"I hope I hurt you, and why won't you shower? You're gagging me."

"I would shower with you."

"Go to hell Bill."

"I still want your phone number."

"If I give it to you, will you leave me alone?"

"Sure."

I wrote the phone number of the local sheriff's department on a piece of scrap paper and handed it to the stinky, injured moron. He ran off like I gave him a prize.

Mark was blasting his horn, waiting for me. I reluctantly got into the passenger side and took a quick look around the cab just in case there's rope, handcuffs, whips, or a gun nearby. I don't trust this guy. Mark was wearing Old Spice aftershave. It was nice to have that in my nose. It's a favorite scent, but I wasn't going to tell him that.

Mark was animated. He shouted aloud that he was finally rid of his brother-in-law, who got a job and moved out. He was smiling ear to ear for a minute or two, then his mood changed. No surprise at all when he brought up New Jersey; he couldn't stand not knowing.

"So just how lost were you?"

"When was I lost?" I said, playing the game.

"New Jersey, remember? When I directed you off the exit for the meat market."

"Oh that, I took the exit as you directed. There was a gas station on the far side of the street with a wide curb. I drove around the block, then parked in front of the gas station, and used their phone. Turned out I was less than fifteen minutes from the place. I eased the truck back on the highway and got there just fine."

"That was it? I mean, you didn't drive around for hours in a panic?"

"Should I have? That doesn't sound very professional."

Mark dropped the subject as we headed down the two-lane highway toward the restaurant. The landscape was dotted with farms and fences, houses, and trees.

There was a mixture of old square farmhouses and beautiful modern ranch-style homes. The sun was beaming, making the day picture perfect. Mark slowed down and drove right past a busy restaurant. He pulled into the driveway of a hotel next door with a shitty grin on his face. The driveway for the hotel had an upward incline which caught my attention.

"What's going on?" I asked, knowing that I just got hustled.

"I told you what women are good for, and I want payment for baby-sitting you."

Mark pulled the emergency brake handle to park, then he slid out the door and disappeared inside to book a room. To my amazement and unbelief, he left the engine running. What great luck! Quickly, I scooted over on his bench style seat. I was going to have to be quiet, a tricky feat with a six cylinder 402 needing a muffler. That was my best guess with the power this truck had. The transmission was in neutral. He had a three on the tree. I slid across Mark's seat and released the emergency brake handle. Keeping it in neutral, I gently braked while guiding the truck down the sloped driveway. It was a cinch to maneuver the truck in the proper direction onto the road past the driveway.

No traffic was in sight. I pushed in the clutch, then pulled the lever toward me, then down into first gear. I had to do this quickly. I noticed a couple of things right away; his gas gauge was close to empty, and a large group of keys were hanging from the ignition. The engine came to life fast and loud when I put the pedal to the metal.

Just as fast, I clutched again and slid the lever past neutral, then forward and straight up into second gear. Third gear was straight down from second. I am doing 70 mph before slowing down a bit, leaving Mark and his hotel idea far behind.

While driving back to the yard, my mind goes back in time to Avery and her boyfriend, Garrett. He had one of these same Chevy three on the tree pickup trucks. We would ride around town on Saturday nights listening to our favorite eight tracks of Deep Purple, Cream, The Guess Who, Rolling Stones, and many more. Of course, this was the mid - late 1970s and having great fun during our high school years.

I would deliberately watch him shift and learned how the transmission worked. Garrett told me it was an H pattern, but on the steering column instead of a center console. Easy. Avery never gave his shift pattern a thought. Garrett broke her heart, even though she knew it couldn't last. He had a dream of being a big city lawyer. Word was that after he graduated law school, he opened a law firm in Dallas, Texas. Avery never saw him again. Pretty certain nobody did.

The terminal was in sight when Mark's pickup sputtered. I limped it to the back of the lot where the loaded trailers were dropped. There was an empty spot between two trailers, about mid-row. This was a great spot to hide a vehicle. I backed it into the spot as far as I could go, then I locked it up with the keys in the ignition. The truck died right at that moment, making me laugh out loud.

It was a stroke of luck that nobody was outside on such a beautiful morning. I jumped in my car and got the heck out of Dodge. The radio station played Dirty Deeds Done Dirt Cheap and a few other favorites while I drove to a restaurant near home. Breakfast was delicious. I sat all by myself with the events of Mark replaying in my head. Eventually, I went home and fully expected a screaming phone call from Brian. It took a half-hour for the call, but it wasn't Brian.

"Hello?"

"Hi Patty, it's Carlos, hey... you turned this place upside down. Mark is seven layers of hell mad at you, saying you stole his truck after breakfast. What in the sam hill happened this morning? And where is Mark's truck?"

"Well, for starters, breakfast didn't happen. Mark drove right past the restaurant and pulled into the hotel next door. He claimed women were only good for screwing and I owed him. He left me alone in his running pickup truck while he went inside to book a room."

"He did that?" Carlos asked, astonished.

"Yes, I guess I was supposed to be obedient and follow him to a room, maybe even give him a striptease, and a blow job first. He never considered that I knew how to drive a three on a tree, or that I would have the guts to leave him there."

"Holy crap! Mark's a bigger idiot than I thought." Carlos said, laughing loudly.

"His pickup truck is in the yard. I parked it between a couple of dropped trailers on the loaded line. I locked the keys inside, and it's out of gas."

Carlos shrieked in laughter. I could hear Mark hollering and throwing things in the driver's room.

"Hang on a second Patty.... hey, you stupid fuck, she parked your truck in the row of trailers! She didn't steal it; she used it to escape being raped by you! And for the record, I am not finished with you yet. That's right, go ahead and run out the door, you coward!"

Mark ran out screaming and cursing, slamming the door hard.

"Good riddance," Carlos said with a giggle. "I called to tell you that Brian has two loads of boxed meat going to Boston. They will be here early Wednesday, and we will deliver them Thursday night. I asked Brian for both loads and he won't cross me. We will leave out Wednesday, say around 4 pm. Oh, and bring extra money, we will have toll roads."

"Yes, I will bring plenty of money. "

It was great having the rest of Monday, Tuesday, and half of Wednesday off. I was curious why Carlos didn't want to leave out Wednesday morning when the loads were due in? We both could have had a good night's sleep in Boston before unloading and been legal on our logs. I should have pressed it, but I barely knew Carlos and let it go, which I would later regret.

Our call ended, and I saw my neighbor Zachary outside, working on his porch railing. His house was next door. The sun was out, and the warm spring breeze felt nice.

"Hey Zach, how are you?"

"Hi Patty, how have you been? I hardly ever see you. What's up?"

"I am good. Work is busy. I just wanted to say thank you for looking after my place and collecting my mail while I am gone all week. I appreciate that."

"Not a problem at all, my pleasure. I have been meaning to ask you if you would you like to have lunch with me sometime?"

"That sounds wonderful Zach. I would love that. Do you want to make it dinner? I am off until Wednesday afternoon."

"Sure! Zach said. I will make my famous lasagna tomorrow. Does 5 pm sound good?"

"I can't wait. The garlic bread is on me."

We both exchanged some more small talk. Zach was not only a local police officer, very handsome and available, but he was also one in a million neighbors that you could trust with your house keys. I had plenty to do between now and our date. I shopped for a new dress and shoes and even got a haircut.

We both exchanged some more small talk. Zach was not only a local police officer, very handsome and available, but he was also one in a million neighbors that you could trust with your house keys. I had plenty to do between now and our date. I shopped for a new dress and shoes and even got a haircut.

"Wow, you look incredible," Zach said, as he opened the door to his two-bedroom bungalow. The delicious smell of his homemade lasagna made my stomach growl. His house was immaculate, with leather furnishings, a couple of nice vases and pictures of tigers on the wall. Very masculine decor. He fixed us cocktails before dinner, and we talked about his life.

"I had a high school sweetheart who was the love of my life. Her name was Beth. We were all set to be married and start our life together. Our plans were set in stone, or so I thought. She blindsided me by asking to take a vacation in Jamaica at a fancy resort with her three girlfriends a couple of months before our wedding. The women were to be her bridesmaids. That trip was supposed to be our honeymoon destination." Zach lowered his head like he was blaming himself. "Beth stood me up at the altar. She literally didn't show up for the wedding that we had planned right down to the flavor of the cake. She embarrassed me in front of 200 guests and our families. Beth had the guts to show up at my doorway late one night, seven months after our wedding was supposed to happen, asking for forgiveness and a chance to start over. She was well along in her pregnancy. She couldn't believe that I already knew. I couldn't forgive her, not yet anyway, and I'm not sure if ever."

"Zach, I am so sorry for the heartbreak you endured. I'm sure it was very painful for you. How could she do that?"

"Her best friend told me that not long after they landed and were settled into the resort, it came to light that Beth had been a pen pal with a man in Jamaica for months. Evidently, this was a planned hook-up. The three women were so angry at Beth that they almost abandoned her there. It didn't take too long after they all returned for Beth to discover she was pregnant."

"Wow, that was cold of her. How did she become a pen pal with a guy in Jamaica?"

"Her sister is a high school teacher. She had a couple of exchange students from the island in her class. They thought it would be a good idea to contact their home school and help to arrange a pen-pal program. Somehow, a parent or big brother to a student was writing to Beth. She loved the attention. Turned out he worked at a fancy, high-end resort."

"The entire trip makes sense now. That was so cruel. I wonder how she could hurt you like that. Beth threw her entire future away for a stranger." I remarked.

"If Beth had come to me, I would have been willing to forgive her. We could have sat down together and figured out what to do with her pregnancy and go ahead with our wedding. I loved her that much. Time is supposed to heal. It's been well over a year since she came over to beg my forgiveness. I am trying to move on. It's so hard to feel better."

Zack looked at me and smiled. It was a broken-hearted smile that nearly broke my heart into a million pieces.

"How long had you two been together?"

"We met in junior high school, and we were a pair until she stood me up. So that would be half our lives. I am 28 now."

"You should find a way back to Beth. She must be so upset and embarrassed by what she has done. Humans screw up, that's what we do. Some of us even screw up a lot. What did she do with her child? He or she would be nearly a toddler by now."

"Beth said something about her sister wanting to adopt the baby. She and her husband had been trying to conceive, but with no luck. I heard she had a Jamaican black baby boy."

"Actually, that's a beautiful skin tone. He will be a handsome guy." I said, grinning.

Zach gave me an irritated side-eye glance, then he announced dinner was ready. We shared a large salad, the garlic bread I brought, and his delicious, extra cheesy lasagna.

Zach asked me about being a trucker, so I brought up Emmett, how awful that job was and how worried he was about my safety. Zach asked me if I had trouble with the men I worked with.

Of course, I had to tell him about Mark's terrible plan and the pickup truck escape. Zach wasn't happy hearing this, but I assured him I would never have allowed this to happen.

Bill also came up because I disliked him so much and thought Zach might have some helpful advice.

"I will come up with the perfect solution," Zach promised. "Act like you are interested. Get him all revved up without letting him get too close to you. I mean, stay safe from this guy. I will figure out how we will knock him down. I will have a plan for Bill."

~ ~

Chapter Six

Trip To Boston with Carlos

The terminal was relatively quiet when I pulled in at 4 pm. Brian was busy on the phone and there was a note with my paperwork saying the shop did the service on my truck. I didn't have any problems to fix. It was just an oil change and lube. Carlos pulled in, driving a cream Delta 88 four-door sedan. He drove right up to my tractor to greet me right in the middle of me, putting my bags and junk in the truck. He rolled down his window to talk.

"Wow Carlos, you have a rocket 88. I have seen this car here, but I wasn't sure who it belonged to."

Carlos laughed. "I needed a big family car. My wife and I are planning on having more kids. Give me a few minutes to pack up, then we can grab our trailers." We hooked up and did our pre-trip inspections. We checked the reefer temps, perfect at minus ten. Our reefer fuel tanks were nearly full, and we rolled out.

"Today was a beautiful day," Carlos said after he keyed up the mike. "Do you have a CB handle yet?"

"No, I can't think of any to choose. What's yours?"

"They call me 'The Bull'. My great-grandfather was a bullfighting champion in Mexico City in the late 1800s. My father and mother came to the United States in the 1940s and became citizens a few years later. I have one younger brother and two sisters. We helped our parents learn English. That was their toughest challenge of all. We are very proud of them."

A driver keyed up, "get off channel 19 if yer gonna jabber jaw."

"Okay, we're so sorry. Hey Patty, go up to channel 28."

"Done."

"Have you been to Mexico? Have you seen any bullfights?" I asked, intrigued.

"Yes, we have been back home a few times. My grandfather passed away over a decade ago. I still have family there, but this is my home."

"You could fight bulls, Carlos. You are about 6 feet 3 inches, 280 pounds, and maybe two percent body fat?"

"Carlos laughed, yes you nailed me!"

The two-lane road from the terminal eventually took us to the highway, then we connected to the toll road and headed east to Boston. We drove across Ohio talking about how the industry mistreats drivers. How we don't get enough rest and pull mostly junk trailers.

"One day, we will ride on something better than springs." Carlos said.

"Like what?" I asked.

"There is talk of future air bags to help support our tractors and trailers. That would go a long way to prevent cargo damage, not to mention back aches."

"I can't picture it, but that would be pretty amazing."

We rode in silence for a long time before Carlos piped up again.

"I try to take my breaks no matter how much Brian pressures me. But sometimes a guy feels great and wants to run the entire distance. Always remember that no job is worth your life, so stop and rest if you are tired. The firing threats are empty. They need us more than we need them."

"Well Carlos, if you really felt that way, we would have left this morning. Now we have to push a lot harder to get there and then, not get our breaks."

"I suppose you are right. We should have left earlier." Carlos said, not sounding one bit sincere.

Carlos and I are talking about this and that and nothing in particular until another topic crosses his mind.

"Do you understand truck grades?"

"Somewhat. I have been down a few."

"Grades are measured in 100 feet units. If you climb or descend 6 feet in a distance of 100 feet, that's a 6% grade. An 8-foot ascent or descent in 100 feet is an 8% grade and so on. That doesn't sound like a big deal, but a 10% downhill grade or higher is significant and can be dangerous or deadly if you are driving too fast."

"Understood."

"If a driver tells you to put your truck into Georgia overdrive, shut your radio off. That guy's an idiot."

"What's that?" I asked.

"Georgia overdrive means you run down a steep grade in neutral, gaining as much speed as possible just to get a thrill."

"Wow, thank you for explaining that. I don't understand why that would be fun. Sounds a lot like suicide. I bet there have been some awful crashes."

"Yes, there are many stories out there. Everything from logging trucks crashing into the side of a mountain to avoid a school bus or trucks with brakes on fire screaming down a hill out of control. There have been drivers able to ride it out on the shoulder and eventually stop once the road begins another climb, and others aren't so lucky. Speed, lack of training and poorly adjusted brakes all play a part."

"Good to know these things. What brought all this up?" I asked.

"We were all at the yard a day or so ago talking with Gabe. He was telling us about a crash he heard about during his trip back from a west coast run. Folks on the CB were talking about a recent out-of-control truck heading down a mountain in Colorado. Evidently, this guy tried to use the guard rail to slow down, but he crashed through and barreled right over the edge. Guess it's still on my mind."

"Oh, that's terrible. Sorry he didn't make it down."

"Yea, me too." Carlos said with a sigh.

I lightened things up. "So, who haven't I met yet?"

"Well, hmmm. Have you met Arlo, Sam, or Billy?"

"You mean stinky Bill?"

"No, Billy. He used to run a cattle truck. He walks with a pronounced limp, but he refuses to talk about what happened. Arlo is just a regular guy, married with a couple of kids, and Sam is divorced, childless, and trying to save for his next new toy. He is into muscle cars."

"I bet his x-wife didn't appreciate his passion."

"Exactly. He hardly ever talks about her. He says life is too short to be miserable."

"He needed to do what he felt was best."

"We all know that Roger has been a bit rough with you, but did you know he was a medic in Vietnam?"

"No way, but I guess thinking about it, he stands straight and carries himself well. Roger apologized to me and promised to help if I needed any. He has stopped being an ass."

"That's great to hear. He needed to be a better man right from the start." Carlos said.

"I am sure I left out a few more of us. You will eventually meet everyone. Ron mentioned to me not too long ago that he was hiring a few more drivers. He didn't elaborate."

We ran out of things to talk about and went back down to channel 19. Traffic was moderate.

Carlos and I were motoring along with the sunset in our mirrors, almost out of Ohio, when BOOM he blew a left rear trailer tire right in front of me. A flame shot from the tire and the gator spun off in the middle of the road. I quickly veered right and missed it.

"We'll crap." Carlos said.

"Yea, I saw it blow and about jumped out of my skin."

"Me too."

"You left a gator on the road."

"Yes, I am going to get off the highway the best I can."

Carlos exited a couple of miles ahead at the next ramp to ensure his and the tire man's safety from traffic. The blown tire was on the highway side.

"Go on up to Harborcreek, just past Erie, and wait for me there. It's a decent truck stop. It may take me a while to get a service truck."

"Okay, will do." I said.

The truck stop Carlos sent me to was large. There were parking spots available even though it was late evening. There were some beautiful trucks here. I parked between a gorgeous light blue Western Star and a GMC (Jimmy) that had a rough idle and was blowing smoke out the stacks. GMC trucks with the famous 60 series Detroit Diesel engines had problems. Aside from rough idling and inefficiencies, they were tough to start in the cold and known for oil leaks. Even with their problems, GMC was a popular truck.

I saw a couple of Mack trucks parked across the lot, and I thought of Maggie. She probably ended up in a scrap yard. There was nothing left of her to save. Her hey-days were over a very long time ago. I walked inside to use the restroom and then went back out to my truck and checked my reefer; it was holding at minus ten. I laid down on my bunk and fell sound asleep.

There was a knock on my door that startled me awake. It was the middle of the night. I jumped up, still dressed minus my boots.

"Get up Patty, let's get breakfast. I am starving." Carlos said.

"Sure," I answered, reaching for a comb to look presentable, then I laced up my boots and slid my coin purse into my jeans pocket. "Hang on a second. I need to grab my clean-up bag. I have furry teeth."

Carlos stood quietly and waited for me to climb out of my truck.

"Did you get some rest?" I asked while we walked inside.

"Yes, I napped a bit, waiting for the tire guy. He brought the wrong tire, so he had to go back to his shop for the correct one. He took a long time to return. I am all fixed now."

When I came out of the bathroom, Carlos was playing on a machine, trying to grab a toy with a big claw.

"I almost won." Carlos said with a chuckle.

"You might win the two-dollar toy after feeding the machine twenty bucks."

Carlos nodded. We sat down in an empty dining room. There was one guy sitting at the counter, leaning over a cup, smoking a cigarette. I wondered if he had been there all night. A sleepy night server brought only one glass of water to our table.

"Excuse me, sir, but you cannot bring the lizards inside. She must leave."

Carlos just stared at her for a moment. "Are you for real, miss? This young lady is my friend and co-worker. I find your attitude extremely offensive."

"Well, you shoulda said you were teaming."

"None of your business, ma'am."

The server firmly set down a second water glass, purposefully spilling some of it. She gave me a hateful look, then took our orders. We both had biscuits and gravy served up with coffee and plenty of nasty attitude. She disappeared and never refilled our cups. I walked over to the coffee station and brought the steamy pot to our table.

"Don't you dare leave her a tip," Carlos said.

"Wasn't going to."

We finished our breakfast, and Carlos dropped a penny into his water glass. We paid for our food and walked outside into a warm night breeze. "Look up," Carlos said.

What an amazing sky! Zillions of sparkling stars overhead. We stood there in awe, taking in the universe. I could have stood there for hours. It was such a beautiful night sky. We were picking out the constellations together.

"Do think we are alone?" Carlos asked.

"No, I think there are all kinds of life out there."

"Yes, I agree," Carlos said, still looking up at that brilliant sky with a perfect half-moon. Carlos paused like he had a lot to say on the topic, but he decided not to.

We did a quick walk around our trucks and caught up our logbooks. At the last minute, we topped off our fuel. "It's better to be safe than sorry, oh, and put your reefer into defrost mode. These units can freeze up and stop working." Carlos remarked.

"Done."

It was only a handful of miles until we saw the Welcome to New York sign. We had about 500 miles left to reach Boston and we're still on track to deliver later today.

We stayed on channel 19. There were random smokey bear reports and the occasional conversation that faded in and out. Pre-dawn traffic was light. The lights of my dash were illuminating my interior as we rolled along the New York thruway. I found the switch and dimmed them a bit. Our engines were humming along perfectly, with some added road noise from the tires.

We were halfway between Rochester and Syracuse in the Finger Lakes region when we saw a big plume of dirt and debris coming towards us.

"Brake hard and pull over fast!" Carlos shouted in a panic.

It's really tough to bring a loaded truck to a quick stop. We put our four-way flashers on to alert traffic. Then we braked hard, badly smoking them, and skidded onto the shoulder. We were completely away from the travel lanes. The westbound truck was barreling directly towards us, on its side, coming across the median. The loud boom and crash of a truck falling apart was alarming. The crashed truck, along with dirt and debris, came to rest half-way into the left lane.

"Oh, my dear Jesus, Carlos. What just happened?"

Carlos didn't hear me. He had already jumped out to see if he could help the driver. I was shaken up a bit, but after a minute, I climbed out of my truck and jogged over to Carlos, who was assessing how to get the injured guy out of his truck. The only plausible way was through his busted-out windshield. By now, there was a line of trucks that had pulled over to assist. Other drivers were running over to help, and they got the man safely out and onto a grassy spot. The driver was lucky to be alive. He had gashes on his face from the broken glass, the left side of his head was hamburger, and his ear was mostly ripped off. It looked like he had a broken arm. Those were just the visible injuries. Someone was wrapping the guy's head in a towel to help stop the bleeding. Somebody somewhere got to a phone and called for help. Many police cars showed up and the ambulance soon arrived. Traffic could creep through the gap between us and the crashed truck, but it was making everyone uneasy. The highway patrol quickly closed the highway behind us. Since we weren't involved, we could leave the scene.

His truck was a cabover Freightliner much like ours. He was pulling a dry van, which was destroyed. It seems like trucks always crash driver side down. No explanation why, but it's a thing. We pulled back onto the New York thruway, still plenty shook up.

"Hey Carlos, go back up to channel 28."

"Okay."

"What the heck is going on? That was so scary! First a blown tire, then we witnessed a nasty crash. Let's change the negative energy to positive by telling cheerful stories," I said.

"You go first," Carlos said.

"I was a kid when my family still lived in northern Minnesota. My girlfriend and I were about seven or eight years old, and we would have so much fun in the winter. There was a really tall hill near our houses. It had a long, sheer icy drop with a slight ledge about half-way down. We would bundle up in our coats, hats, mittens, and boots and take our ten-dollar wooden toboggans up this big hill, making foot holds with our boots like we were climbing Everest. Once we got to the top, we would go down this thing much like 'Georgia overdrive' as it's called and have the fun of our lives. Remember the ledge? We would hit that and be airborne the rest of the way down, then we would hit the bottom of this sheer drop and sled for quite a way with just momentum. The worst part was climbing back up, but when you're a kid, it's all great fun. We would climb up and slide down over and over. One time we even spotted a moose near the woods nearby, but he wasn't interested in us."

"Wow, I never had the chance to experience a northern winter. I think I would have frozen to death. Now I understand why you could drive Maggie with no heat." Carlos said, laughing.

"Maggie nearly froze me to death before spring finally showed up, but it helped a lot being a winter girl. You're up next, Carlos."

"When I was a kid, we would visit relatives back in Mexico City. My uncle would take my brother and I to the City of The Dead. We would try to find Aztec artifacts and cool stuff like that. The most fun of all was visiting every year in November. There were parades and celebrations. October 31st through November 2nd was called Día de los Muertos. There were parades that would feature skeleton puppets, chocolate skulls and moving altars. Traditional dancers would carry marigolds and bread. The food was to die for."

"Hahahaha!! That was funny."

"It isn't a funeral or spooky. It's about joy and color and so much flavor. All in celebration of our deceased ancestors. We would enjoy things like Pan de Muertos, Mole Negro, Chapulines, Pepitorias, Tamales of course, and hot chocolate for us kids. The favorite adult beverage was tequila infused with marigolds. I miss that part of my childhood."

"That sounds like a lot of fun. So, the celebration serves as a bridge between the living and the dead?"

"Exactly."

We talked and laughed while the mile markers ticked past. The starry sky had long since yielded to the morning.

"Are you feeling better, Carlos?"

"Yes, for sure."

We had a quiet ride the rest of the way across New York, only stopping for the occasional toll booth. We were soon past Albany and hopeful that we had broken the negative energy.

"There is a Howard Johnson (known as Ho Jo's) at the first service plaza in Massachusetts. Let's stop there and get something to eat," Carlos said.

"That sounds great. It is coming up on lunchtime. We're making good time, even with the problems we had earlier on." I said, feeling hungry.

We got parked and walked inside. We were both in need of a restroom and then we claimed two empty stools at the counter.

A server, who was both busy and friendly, said hello and handed us menus. Carlos decided we should have the roast beef sandwiches with mashed potatoes. The food was delicious.

"I think we earned an ice cream sundae. Wouldn't you agree?"

"Absolutely."

Carlos ordered the biggest hot fudge sundae they offered.

"Please make mine a small." I requested. The girl nodded.

We finished our desserts, paid for our food, and left her a nice tip. Carlos gave me a big hug outside. "We're only two hours from Boston. Let's get these loads delivered."

Eastern New York and Western Massachusetts were hilly. The New York Mountain ranges are the Catskills and Adirondacks. The Poconos are part of the Appalachian range and run primarily through eastern Pennsylvania. Massachusetts has the Berkshire Mountains and a few others. We had a couple of downhills we had to be careful with, but past that, no issues.

There was already a lot of traffic around Boston that afternoon. It's a major city, with multiple highways and many outlying suburbs. The Boston area branches out in all directions, and the eastern boundary of the city is the coastline. The port of Boston is a major seaport for global freight entering and departing the country.

We pulled into the warehouse parking lot. We were early, but they were happy to see us. Meat is expensive and the meat distributors don't want it on the trucks any longer than necessary. We were assigned doors 4 and 5. Carlos and I slid our jackets on and walked inside to the refrigerated dock.

The receiver greeted us and collected our paperwork. "You both can start pulling off your pallets and stage them over there."

He pointed to the striped area on the dock floor. The pallet jacks were electric, which made for easy unloading. We dropped the dock plates into our trailers, popping them up from the floor with a chain and a hard yank. They made a loud bang as the front edge of the plate dropped into the trailer. We each had 23 pallets of fresh boxed meat on our 48-foot trailers. One pallet was singled in the nose to compensate for the weight of the reefer unit.

Carlos and I were neck and neck getting unloaded. We were empty within an hour. As Carlos and I were pulling off our pallets, the warehouse employee collected them with his regular forklift and put them away. Our bills were signed by the receiver, and we were done. We moved our trucks across the road in a gravel lot. A half dozen trucks were parked there either waiting their turn or they were already empty and needed to finish a break.

"We need to call in and let Brian know we are empty," I said.

"We could always wait until morning. We need to show a break here." Carlos remarked.

"You can do what you want, but I am going to call in," I said, with a bit of impatience.

Carlos followed me inside to the pay phone in the lobby. There was another driver using it. He was having a tearful conversation with his wife and refused to end his call. They went back and forth for what seemed like a long time. The driver was begging her not to leave him, crying and begging. It was heartbreaking to witness. Trucking is probably the number one career that guarantees a divorce, especially if the wife doesn't understand the industry.

"Come on man, we need the phone too," Carlos said to the crying man.

"Fuck off," the driver said to Carlos, then he wiped his snotty nose on his shirt sleeve. Carlos disappeared and showed up a minute later with the receiver, who wasn't having any part of this guy.

"Excuse me, sir," the receiver said in a raised voice, "Can't you read the sign that says we limit calls to three minutes? And absolutely no personal calls?"

"Fuck you, too." The driver said.

The receiver forcefully grabbed the phone out of his hand and slammed it down hard, then he shouted, "GET OUT NOW!"

The startled guy left with no more issues.

Brian picked up on the second ring, Carlos went first.

"Great job getting unloaded. You are picking up at 8 am in Braintree, Mass, just a little south of where you are now. You won't need your reefer. The load delivers in Columbus, Ohio the next day. They are first come, first served."

Brian gave Carlos the load numbers and addresses.

My turn, with Carlos in earshot.

"I see you found Boston without a seeing-eye dog," Brian snapped. I ignored the comment. He didn't remember that he had sent me to Boston twice before this time.

"You are picking up a load near Schenectady, New York, at 9 am and bringing it straight to the yard."

"Okay," I said, then Brian gave me the load number and the name of the company. Then he abruptly slammed the receiver, ending the call.

"Wow! Brian treats you like dog shit."

"He doesn't bother me, but I am figuring out his game. He wants me to drive straight back, then he will force me right back out with no rest to deliver a 'hot load' to someplace that doesn't want an early delivery."

"Brian does that?"

"Absolutely, he does."

"What are you going to do now? We both need to get our trailers washed out."

"There was little to no blood leakage on the trailer floor, so I will cheat a bit and pass on the washout. I am going to head west. I need to figure out where this company is and still have time to get some sleep before loading. Thank you for everything. It's been great running with you, Carlos."

"Can I talk you into hanging out with me for a bit longer? We can head down to the harbor and buy some fresh catch from a food truck. There is nothing more delicious."

"Thank you for the offer, Carlos. I will take a rain check on that. I need to roll out of here."

We said our goodbyes. I traveled back to New York before stopping at a service plaza to catch up on my logbook. It was way behind, and I needed to show a break in Boston to be legal. I will re-do my log pages over the weekend, and then I will be back on track. I felt immense regret for not leaving yesterday morning.

Before I left the plaza, I made a call from a pay phone to directory service to see if I could track down this company. The operator did, in fact, have a phone number and I asked her if there was an address with the number. I had the luck of the Irish when she gave me both. The operator dialed the company, and the lady who picked up was pleasant and she was happy to give me directions. Best of all, she said I could sleep on their property. That was a home run.

On the way there, I found a truck stop where I could sit still, shower, and unwind. I parked, then went inside and found a friendly counter girl. I paid the ten-dollar shower fee for a ratty towel that I will place on the floor in front of the sink to stand on and a door key. The shower was small, and most are. The shower was great and the flowery scent of my shampoo and soap was relaxing.

I felt like a new person after cleaning up and was thankful this truck stop had hot water.

I took my bags back out to the truck, then made my way back inside to the restaurant and found a corner table. The server was busy running here and there, so I ordered the buffet and a cup of coffee. I needed nothing else, so I left her alone. From the truck stop, I made my way to the customer and enjoyed a good night's sleep.

They loaded me right on schedule. Brian didn't say I needed my reefer on, and it turned out I didn't. The trip back was uneventful. That's trucking at its best. Just us drivers motoring down the highways and byways minding our own business and having a great time. I was rested and felt amazing, so I drove the entire 700 miles back. It was pitch dark when I arrived at the terminal. Instead of checking in with Larry, I sat the trailer down on the loaded pad and put the bills in the overnight drop box. I parked my tractor, grabbed my bags and dirty laundry, then climbed into my car. I leaned my head back against the headrest for a couple of minutes to breathe a long sigh of relief. My head was pounding as thoughts about that crash kept replaying. Carlos had made the wrong decision. If we had time to stop, we certainly had time to hammer down and get past him before he crossed the median. I realize he was only trying to keep me safe but stopping like that was very hard on the equipment and put us both in far more danger.

This is just my opinion, and I never brought it up. Heavy fatigue washed over me during my hours' drive home. I was in a sleep coma by 11 pm.

~ ~

Chapter Seven

An Eventful Weekend

My weekend was wide open. I woke up Saturday morning feeling better and thinking that I had something to do. Oh yes, it was little Chrissy's fourth birthday. I ring Avery to ask when the party starts.

"Oh, just come over anytime today!" Avery said, excited.

"Okay, I will be there this afternoon." I hurried up and did my laundry and then went shopping for a toy and an outfit suitable for a four-year-old. Avery's house was a simple A-frame in town. It was a cute house in a nice neighborhood. I squeezed my Toyota onto the edge of her packed driveway. I got to see Avery's mom, whom I hadn't seen in a while. Lots of family and friends came and went and fussed over the birthday girl. There were quite a few people coming and going. Chrissy was over the moon with excitement. Avery served punch and sandwiches, cookies, and candies. There were tons of balloons and toys everywhere. The large, pink frosted chocolate cake had a My Pretty Pony theme served with two kinds of ice-cream. Avery was thrilled I had shown up. After two hours, I couldn't handle anymore, so I made an excuse and left.

My place was across town. I pulled into my driveway and saw a note on my door. It was from Zach; he wrote that a colleague had called in sick this morning, so he had to cover. This was a gift because I needed to rest and decompress. He also invited me to a buffet at noon tomorrow if I was still home.

My place was a tiny, rented house with meager furnishings, but it was perfect for me. I got what I needed from a couple of estate sales and scrounging. My favorite piece of furniture was a cozy chair that I could recline on. I made myself a cup of hot chocolate, then I wrapped up in a favorite throw and fell sound asleep. My nap was short-lived. The phone jangled me awake.

"Hello?"

"Hi Pat, it's your ol' dad here. I was wondering how the new job has been going?"

"It's been going well so far. Not too many issues other than taking the wrong exit in New Jersey a while back, and then having to fork over money to get some guy to move his car, which was totally necessary to get myself out of that predicament. And this week I ran to Boston with another driver, and he mentioned something interesting. Have you heard any talk about airbags instead of springs underneath trucks and trailers?"

"Yes, there is talk out there about that. The industry is trying to figure it out because of so much cargo damage. There are changes coming."

"That would make everything better. I hope that happens. It would be a great leap forward."

"Yes, it would," Dad said in agreement.

"Past that, I am having a bit of trouble with a smelly driver who won't leave me alone. He is a big problem, and I feel like I have to look over my shoulder every time I am at the yard."

"You better get a handle on that driver. Don't let him get the upper hand."

"Definitely," I answered, really wishing I could go back to sleep.

"Anyway, the reason I called is to tell you a story I heard about a friend of a friend who is an owner-operator. Word is that another trucker had attempted to steal his fuel while he was parked at the far side of a customer in N. Carolina because he didn't want to listen to everyone else's truck idling all night. I guess this wasn't the first time that someone tried to steal his fuel. He got insanely pissed at the guy who was right in the middle of removing his fuel cap and standing ready with a siphon hose. The thief probably didn't realize anyone was in the truck. Stupid assumption, right? Anyway, the owner-op came charging out of his truck with a gun and, in a fit of rage, demanded that guy's truck keys. The guy grudgingly surrendered his keys after a lot of kicking and screaming and threats of being shot. The owner-op then positioned his truck in front of the thief's truck. Then he put it in fast reverse, slamming his trailer hard into the thief's front end at least twice, crushing it, and busting his radiator. Fortunately, the owner-op's trailer had been fortified with extra heavy gauge steel shortly after he bought it. After that, he calmly got out of his cab and tossed the keys back to the thief, who was screaming bloody murder. The owner-op moved to a different parking spot on the other side of the customer where the other waiting trucks were parked. My friend said this guy went right back to bed as if this was just normal. I was totally impressed," Dad said, between fits of uproarious laughter.

"Wow, I can only imagine how surprised that thief must have been. I would have loved to hear what explanation he gave to the tow truck driver. Anyway, why would someone steal fuel?" I asked in all my naivety.

"Fuel theft is a huge problem industry wide. Company drivers like yourself don't give it a thought because they issued you a fuel card. Your company pays for your fuel. There is a percentage of owner operators and lease operators who consider all of their earnings to be profit. They don't want to spend their profit to buy fuel, even though it's an essential part of doing business. They want to steal your fuel. The cost is several hundred dollars a week in fuel to operate a truck. I am certainly not saying this is okay. Unfortunately, stealing will continue as long as big rigs are on the road, and it's not just fuel. Some guys will take literally anything not tied down. Please understand that it's only a percentage thing. Most owner-operators are honest and decent."

All I could manage to say was, "Wow."

Dad continued, "Not too long ago, I heard a story from a driver friend who applied to work for a guy who owned three trucks. After the interview, the owner briefly excused himself before returning with a siphon hose and pump. He extended the hose and pump, then boldly asked the guy if he could do this for him. That driver immediately got red-faced angry and said he would never steal fuel or anything else for that matter, and he had a lot of guts asking him to do that. The owner said he couldn't hire him. The guy said that was fine because he was no longer interested in the job."

"That's crazy. I think most drivers out here would have told him the same thing."

"Yes, I totally agree," Dad said.

We chit-chatted a little longer, then we said our goodbyes. It was great hearing from Dad, but I was exhausted and went straight to bed.

I woke up Sunday morning feeling much better. The week was behind me, and it could stay there. Zach mentioned coming up with a plan for Bill. He wants me to be friendly with that slob, and I am not one bit willing to comply. We will most definitely discuss this over lunch.

The outfit I chose for lunch was jeans and a nice blouse. Zach rang my doorbell at exactly noon, wearing dress pants and a turquoise shirt.

"Hi Zach, you're looking dapper."

"Dapper? He laughed, sounds like you are from the English countryside. Let's go eat."

Zach took us to the same restaurant where I had breakfast after my brush with Mark and his wild idea. They have great food and as we walked in, the delicious smell of the entrees and pastries made us hungry. We were seated after ten minutes. Not a terrible wait for a table at a packed restaurant.

The lunch buffet, which was a huge Sunday spread, featured everything from chicken and steak to crab legs and salmon, plus a gigantic salad bar and a dozen bread choices. We filled our plates eager to dig in.

"How was your week?" Zach asked me between bites.

"I had a busy trip running to Boston with a driver friend named Carlos," I said.

"Tell me what happened," Zach asked, interested.

"We were motoring along towards the east coast when a few drivers keyed up and talked a lot about nothing. Carlos ended up with a trailer tire blowing out not too far from Erie, Pa. After he got repaired, we had breakfast at a truck stop not too far from his blow out. After we got rolling again, we talked about childhood stuff, nothing all that exciting. We made it to Boston on time."

"Do you remember telling me that Emmett warned you to be careful? He told you that the other drivers are really not your friend?" Zach sounded jealous, which gave me an instant headache.

"Absolutely, and Carlos was a zero threat. By the way, he is a nice friend and co-worker."

There was a long silence while we ate, and then I decided this was a good time to bring up my concerns.

"Zach, I need to ask you what I am supposed to do with Bill. Last time I saw him, he pinned me against my truck and started humping my ass. That guy is beyond disgusting."

Zach laughed so hard. "I am glad you asked me. I came up with a brilliant plan. He doesn't know where you live, right?"

"Right."

"You are going to sucker him in. I need him to call you, thinking he is going to get lucky. Give him your number in a flirty way."

"I would rather set him on fire."

"Well, don't do that. I would have to arrest you."

"Our mayor lives on the north side of town, close to the boondocks. His enormous, pillared house is an immaculate showplace with flower gardens and pristine fountains that double as bird sanctuaries. He has a curved paved driveway that goes past the guest house, which sits behind the main house. Where I am going with all of this is the fact that our fine mayor hates trucks."

"Why?" I asked.

"He was talking at a town hall meeting a while back about the time he had a flat tire. He was trying to change it himself on the shoulder. The tucks were whizzing by way too close to him. One trucker even blew his cap across the field. He was hopping mad after that."

"It sounds like he had the right to be upset. Not very many trucks or cars are polite enough to give a guy some room."

That seemed to go right past Zach, and he was grinning like he had the plan of the century.

"So, what's the big reveal?" I asked, then regretted it.

"Here is the plan. You live at least an hour east of where you work, right? So, the likelihood of him driving his car to see you is small. He will, without a doubt, call you to set something up on his way east in the truck if he thinks he has a chance with you. When he calls you, give him the mayor's address and tell him to drive his rig around to the back and blow his horn in front of the guest house. His truck will tear up the flowerbeds and several of the mayor's ornate things."

"What do you have against the mayor? That's vandalism, trespassing, criminal intent to destroy property and half a dozen other charges. And what part of that wouldn't land me in jail along with him? I mean, all Bill would have to say in court is that I instructed him to drive through private property on purpose, intending to cause extensive damage."

"I thought it would be hilarious and teach Bill a lesson."

"Sorry, I am not onboard with this plan of yours."

Zach looked like he just stepped in it big time.

"Okay, maybe that wasn't my best plan."

Our meals were finished. I got up to leave and Zach followed me to settle our bill. We agreed I would cover the tip, and he would pay for our meals. We walked outside into the bright sunlight; I squinted to adjust my eyes.

"Do you want to see a movie or hangout?" Zach asked.

"No, I am good. Tomorrow starts my work week. Actually Zach, without making you angry, I think we make great neighbors, and we probably shouldn't mess with that."

Zach looked uncomfortable, but he seemed to agree.

"Anyway, I was thinking about what you said about Beth wanting to mend things. You could try buying her some beautiful flowers and see what she's been doing. I think she would really like that."

Zach lit up, then he ran his hand through his hair, clearly conflicted. "Do you think that would work? I mean, I have been thinking about her so much. I don't know what to do."

"Absolutely! Unless you take the next step, you won't know if the spark is still there. Go find Beth and see what happens."

Zach agreed. He drove me home with the biggest grin on his face.

~ ~

Chapter Eight

Bill Screwed Up

My phone rang early Monday morning. It was Brian.

"Where were you Friday night? I had you on a load going to Indianapolis."

I took the phone receiver and banged it hard several times on the countertop.

"Bad connection. Talk to me when you decide to be reasonable."

Brian started screaming something incoherent, so I hung up on him. Thirty minutes passed before he called back. He was nicer this time.

"Can you please take a load to Indianapolis later today?"

"Sure, I can be there at noon. Will that work?"

"I guess so." BAM, he loudly hung up.

There was a lot of activity at the yard when I showed up mid-morning. Jeff was at the dispatch window arguing with Brian about getting time off. He explained his grandmother had passed away over the weekend, and she lived down in Alabama. Brian was trying to deny Jeff time off, but Jeff yelled loud enough to bring Ron out of his office.

"Brian, you don't have the authority to take Jeff's bereavement time away. You have a load on your board going down to Selma, Alabama. You will give him that load, plus the rest of the week off."

"But I had someone else on that run." Brian tried to argue with no luck.

"It's Jeff's run."

"Fine, then!"

"Thank you, Ron," Jeff said, then he turned to leave and nearly bumped into me.

"Oh, hi Patty, how are things?"

"Things couldn't be better. Thanks for asking." I said, smiling while Brian stared daggers at both of us. I am sorry you lost your grandma. We both sat down at a table.

"Thank you. She was fantastic. I just wish I could have seen her more often. Thanks to Ron, I can go to her funeral, say my goodbyes, and be with my family."

We talked a bit more and then Jeff excused himself and left. He was eager to head south. Leroy was standing near the payphone talking to Marty. They were laughing and talking about a car full of girls, perhaps freshmen in college. A couple of them had flashed Marty, and he was giggling up a storm, not being shy at all.

"One girl was a beautiful blond. I couldn't believe it when she raised up her top and those beautiful gonzagas fell right out! Then I got flashed by another one, who was sitting in the back seat. There were four of them in the car. It was a great view! I wanted to get a handful of those beautiful boobies."

Marty was making up and down hand gestures that were hilarious. Leroy was grinning and enjoying the visual of the story.

"I got flashed a while back, too. It's always a great day when the ladies show off like that," Leroy said. They talked a few more minutes about work and stuff.

Eleanor came out to say hello. Harold was right behind her, trying to look up her skirt.

"Do you mind Harold? Please stop acting like this towards me and Lisa!"

"As long as I don't touch, I am free to look at the merchandise. Office women are a dime a dozen." Harold scoffed, then he left, much to our relief.

"Hello Eleanor, I feel your pain with that issue. Harold is a terrible human being. When Bill and Roger come after me, I do my best to ignore them and let their comments slide off my back. The other drivers are polite and kind. Those two won't stop."

"Harold won't stop either. It seems we have no recourse. I need this job. What can we do? Office women are nobody. Sorry, enough of that. I need your logs for last week if you have them."

"I do. They are in my truck. I will go get them."

Just my luck, Bill comes out of nowhere and comes trotting over to my truck like a starved dog, complete with his usual stench. I had just grabbed my paperwork and was locking my truck.

"What do you want, Bill?"

"I want you, of course."

His bad breath nearly knocked me backward. "Why can't you clean up like a normal person?"

"You gag everyone you get close to. Please stay away from me!"

It was a warm summer day with a pleasant breeze, which helped to diffuse the stench. Bill was oblivious to everything around him and made the mistake of grabbing my arm in an attempt to drag me to God knows where. His grip was iron tight. I screamed and yelled at the top of my lungs. Eleanor joined Ron, and they both came out running. Ron screamed, "Drop her NOW!"

Bill realized his mistake and quickly let go. I fell hard to the ground and was momentarily stunned. My arm was hot and stinging where he held his grip.

Ron was furious. "How dare you grab Patty like that! You have no right to assault her or any other driver! My office now!"

Eleanor and I were both startled. I brushed myself off and handed her my paperwork, which was now a little crumpled. Eleanor and I sat together at the picnic table until she felt confident that I was okay. Bill emerged five minutes later, carrying a bucket of hot water, soap, and rags. He was heading to his truck, cursing and raging. A minute after that, Ron came back outside to join us. He sat down with a heavy sigh.

"I have been wanting an excuse to fire Bill for a while now. I told him that if his truck wasn't as clean as new, I would bring sexual assault charges against him. Bill protested until I mentioned the time that I witnessed him grabbing your ass. I started to walk over to help you then, but you took care of the situation. Honestly, I owe you an apology for not dealing with him sooner. I also spoke with Mark the other day and gave him the opportunity to apologize for taking you to the hotel instead of breakfast. He said that women should be at home, and he didn't feel bad about his actions. He said he couldn't believe you knew how to drive his pickup truck. That part was hilarious, and it took all I had not to bust out laughing. I told him that unless he apologized to you, he could no longer work here. The safety of my employees comes first. He refused and quit right on the spot."

"Wow, that's a lot to unpack," I said, surprised. Eleanor looked shocked, too.

"I can't have drivers that pose a threat to you or anyone else."

"I accept your apology, Ron. I think Bill has been a problem for all of us lately. Thank you for standing up for me. I appreciate it."

"Is there anything else I can help you with? I haven't talked to you about your work lately," Ron asked.

"Actually, there are two things you can help with. The first one is how Harold treats the office women, and the second one is Brian's mistreatment of me and his obvious contempt. He is still trying to figure out ways to make me quit."

Eleanor piped up, "Harold is so terrible to Lisa and me. We don't know how to make him stop. He all but shakes his junk at us and demands that we allow him to look down our shirts and up our skirts. We are at our wits' end." Eleanor was near tears at this point.

Ron looked irritated. "Brian and I will have a discussion concerning his attitude. And about Harold, I can't fire him because the owner hired him. There is a corporate meeting coming up in a few days. If you and Lisa will compile a folder about his mistreatment and sexual harassment, I will be happy to present it at the meeting. The owner is fair, and I am confident that he won't tolerate this behavior."

We both thanked Ron as he got up from the picnic table.

"Wait a second," Ron said as he turned back to us. "I almost forgot to tell you both that I hired another woman driver. She will be here first thing in the morning. Her name is Melanie, or Mel for short. She will stay at the hotel for the time being. She is another reason I wanted Bill gone. There is way too much liability with his bad behavior."

Ron left us sitting there with a ton of questions. We looked at each other, momentarily stunned, then we walked back inside. Bill's trash pile was now halfway up the side of his truck. He was still raging. This was entirely his problem.

I finally got organized and did that run to Indianapolis. It was a load of parts of some sort going to a factory near the airport. They quickly unloaded me, and then I returned the trailer to the yard. It was coming up on evening and I was surprised to see Carlos there.

"Hey Carlos, guess what?!"

"What?" He asked while walking closer to me. He just finished dropping his trailer a little way down the row from mine.

"Yesterday, Ron informed me and Eleanor that he just hired a new female driver. Her name is Melanie. She starts orientation in the morning."

"No way!" Carlos exclaimed. "You know, we both are going to have to be nosy and show up in the morning. Kind of as a welcoming committee."

"You are just too curious," I said.

"Yes, of course. See you in the morning."

~ ~

Chapter Nine

Melanie

Carlos called me early the next morning and told me to be ready for breakfast. I agreed, and we met up at a restaurant close to work. We discussed many things, including Brian and his ongoing mistreatment. It really upset Carlos, but I assured him it was something that Ron promised to look into. We talked about the new woman driver, and both of us wondered how she would do.

We showed up a few minutes after 10 am to a lot of commotion. News travels fast because everyone who wasn't on a run seemed to be there. We were told that Mel was in Harold's office going over stuff. So, Carlos and I went outside and sat down at the picnic table soaking up summer rays. Leroy, Steve, and a few others wandered outside with us. Ron came outside too, but he did something very unexpected. He walked up behind me and snatched my knife from my back pocket. I don't even know why I brought it. Force of habit, I suppose.

"I have been hearing rumors that you have a really cool weapon. I meant to approach you about it yesterday, but I got sidetracked." Ron said, and then he played with it. Everyone was shocked and surprised, even Carlos looked gob smacked. I was wondering how anyone even knew about it.

"It was a gift from a dear friend. He taught me how to drive and gave me my first job."

"I know. I checked up on you after you applied, and I talked to his nephew John. He said you did a great job for his uncle, despite the job being brutal. John told me to give you a chance but to wait a month or so for your lungs to heal up. Apparently hauling salt isn't so much fun."

Ron continued to play with my knife.

Carlos reached out. "Let me see her knife."

"No way," Ron answered, holding it out of reach. "It's my birthday next month. I would really love to have one of these beauties."

"How about we make a deal? If I get dispatched on fewer floor loads, I will buy you a knife like mine. They have been good for my muscle tone, but they are awful hard on me. It's been a tough weekly endurance marathon."

"Those floor loads weren't supposed to be a thing past your first load. I went round and round with Brian, telling him he was going too far, and to this day, nobody knows how you managed to get that trailer empty, and so fast. That was supposed to be the only one. Heck, this company doesn't deal with floor loads. Brian must be brokering them. I promise you won't be getting those again."

"Thank you, Ron. That would be appreciated. I will turn the world upside down to buy you a knife for your birthday, I promise."

"I will hold you to that, Ron said with a big grin."

Everyone had wandered back inside hoping to get to know Mel. Carlos, Ron, and I were the only ones still outside. I explained how the receiver didn't care for Brian and offered a dozen workers to assist me in stacking all those boxes on pallets and getting me done quickly.

"That was really great of them to help like that," Carlos said. "I wasn't aware Brian tried to scuttle your job."

"Yes, and that load shouldn't have happened," Ron said, irritated.

There was nothing left to say. Ron handed my knife back to me and we went back into the driver's room. Ron disappeared into his office. I handed my knife to Carlos and his face lit up like a kid being handed a new set of Legos. He eagerly played with it.

We spotted Mel talking to Leroy near the pay phone. She was stick thin with gorgeous, shoulder-length blonde hair, big blue eyes and a cigarette hanging off her bottom lip. She appeared to be about 30ish and wearing jeans, extra cute boots and an overly tight t-shirt. Carlos and I walked over to her and introduced ourselves. She was friendly and soaking up a lot of attention. We made small talk and then, of course, Harold came out of his office with a bounce in his step.

I swear he looked in love. He tried every excuse to pull her back into his office.

"I need to go over the run sheets and fuel cards and bla bla bla." Harold said, nearly drooling.

"Oh, sorry Harold, I am waiting for someone to take me on a road test. You already went over everything for now." Mel quickly dismissed Harold, and he left looking like a sad puppy.

Of course, Brian was in earshot and said, "Gabe is taking you out. He will be here in a couple of minutes. Can I get you a coffee or soda while you wait?"

"No, thank you," Mel said.

Gabe walked in just then to get Mel, and they scurried out. Brian looked at Carlos and me and told us to get lost.

"We need our dispatch if you have it," Carlos asked.

Brian shuffled through some paperwork and said he didn't know yet and to call him later that day. Same for me.

"Let's go back outside and wait for Mel. I am not done with her yet," Carlos said.

She and Gabe pulled in about twenty minutes later. Mel was driving. She parked his truck off to the side and climbed out. Carlos waited until she walked closer and then offered for us to all have lunch. There was a pizza joint nearby.

Mel quickly agreed. "Yes, thank you. I am starving." It was noon.

Carlos offered Gabe and Leroy the same invitation. Gabe declined because he had to go out on a run. Leroy accepted; he wasn't going out until later.

The four of us drove to the pizza joint in Carlos's car. Once seated, Mel and Leroy said they were starving, so we ordered two extra-large pizzas with everything they could throw on them. Mel seemed to relax quite a bit. She ordered a beer and the three of us gave her the stink eye.

"Hey what? I am not done with orientation yet."

"Fair enough. Enjoy your brew, Mel," Carlos said.

The rest of us ordered a soft drink.

"I am so hungry. Thank you for inviting me."

"Anytime Mel, actually we are all so curious about how you ended up here?"

"I am not curious, just starving," Leroy said.

"Okay then, it's me and Carlos who are really curious," I said, smiling.

Mel wasn't opening up just yet, so we talked about Brian and Ron and, of course, Harold.

"Yea, he gave me the creeps. I actually thought he was going to grab my ass." She said, then took a big gulp of her beer as we chatted for a bit. The pizzas came, and we all dug in. Mel talked to us halfway through her second glass of beer. About that time, the server collected the empty pizza pans. We sat there eagerly, waiting to hear her story.

"Been dating my boyfriend, Levi, for about a year and a half. He always wanted to drive a truck, so he signed up with a company that trained him for a few weeks, then they turned him loose to drive on his own, or solo, as it's called. Levi would be dispatched out to California, and then he would have to sit for three or four days waiting for a return load. He got this big idea that I should ride with him, so about seven months ago he sweet-talked me into getting my chauffeur's license. After listening to him beg me non-stop, I finally agreed to get my license. I quit my job at the local factory, and away we went. He taught me how to drive over time, but it wasn't easy for me. I could barely drive a 5-speed car, let alone a big truck. I was so intimidated by the size of his semi rig."

"That was a big step in your life. You must have been scared to death." I said.

"I was so completely intimidated and scared. It was hard to learn gears. Finally, after a couple of weeks of practice, I could make it through his ten gears without grinding them to dust."

Carlos gave her an ouch look for the abuse of that transmission.

Mel went on, "Levi got real used to me being in the truck and leaned on me to drive more and more. I was willing to do that after I got comfortable with his transmission and clutch and all that stuff, but the son-of-a-bitch decided I would do 80% of the driving after that point."

She finished her second glass of beer, and we all said a resounding no to her third one. Carlos told the waitress to bring her a soda or ice water. Mel gave us a defeated look, then continued.

"He got real mean to me, yelling and screaming over nothing and I just couldn't keep up driving team without the benefit of the second half of the team."

"Were you paid?" Carlos asked.

"Not much at all, just what little bit he would give me out of his pocket, so I called his company and explained the situation. They were plum mad at my boyfriend and brought us straight back to the terminal from California, empty. They said I was never hired on, and I wasn't authorized to drive their equipment."

We all nodded and said they were right. Your boyfriend was wrong to do this to you, risking their equipment and both of your lives. Carlos, Leroy, and I were all in agreement that he should have had her hired on as a trainee. Mel wasn't sure she wanted to agree with us, but after she thought about it, she said his company had the right to be angry.

"They fired Levi right on the spot and told me to get lost, never to ask them for a job. We broke up after that and he went back to his family in Oklahoma. I still had my apartment in Indiana, but I had to give it up. My aunt and uncle took me in, but after driving for those few months, I wanted to keep on driving and not be a burden. I called a few companies trying to find a driving job. Finally, a company hired me, but the terminal manager said I needed to ride with his son for a month to 'learn how to drive.' They only had six trucks total, and it seemed like a total rat dick company. Okay, fine, I agreed, and met this guy the same day we were sent out on a run."

We were sipping our sodas, totally invested in her story.

"This guy was a very overweight, smelly, disgusting mess, and I was instantly regretting my decision. His name was Albert or Al for short. I was in trouble in a quick hurry because we weren't even fifty miles from the terminal, and he was already asking me to give him a piece of ass."

"I ain't training you for nothin' you stupid bitch." And then he would grab any part of me that suited him.

"What did you do? Could you stop him?" I asked, trying to picture this train wreck.

"I kept telling him no, but I knew it was only a matter of time until he was gonna try to help himself no matter what I said. We made it out to the West Coast for a delivery of something or other and then we were scheduled for a pickup in El Paso, Texas. That load was to be delivered in Michigan. Things were getting rough between us. I finally told him to leave his stinking hands off me. I refused his advances, which made him furious. The only thing that saved me from that slime ball was the fact the truck had bunk beds, I had the top bunk and there was no way he could get his fat ass up there, so he never got what he was after."

Mel had a big grin telling us that part. We all burst out laughing. Leroy laughed so hard that soda came out of his nose.

Mel continued on, "So, we were in west Texas heading back from our pickup in California. My bladder was screaming. We pulled into this remote rest area. I mean, it was full of tumbleweeds and dust blowing everywhere. I was taking a pee and heard Albert release the brakes. I knew he was leaving me there. Oh, Dear God was all I could think of at that moment because my purse, bags and everything was in that stupid truck."

The three of us are sitting there with our hands covering or faces. We were horrified, thinking how awful and unimaginable a moment like that would be.

"Thank God he threw my stuff out of the truck before leaving me there. Luckily, there was a pay phone that actually worked. I called his daddy collect and explained the events of the past two weeks with his stinky ass grabbing son.

"I just can't believe my son would act that way; you must have done something to upset him." "Then his daddy hung up on me. That's it, I was abandoned."

We all spoke up at the same time and asked her, "What happened next?"

"Nothing for a few hours. I just sat on the ground in the dirt and the scorching sun was baking me alive. I didn't know how I was going to get out of that rest area. I was desperately in need of water and a rescue. Those rest areas have no roofs and just stone walls. They are just primitive outhouses."

Mel continued on, "After about three hours, a family pulled in and noticed my plight. The missus walked over to me, and I spilled my guts to her."

"You must come with us." She said, immediately giving me water and handing me some cream for my sunburned skin. She loaded up my stuff and put me in the back seat. I was so lucky."

Carlos spoke up. "How long ago did all this happen, Mel?"

Roughly a month ago, during mid-June. That family was nice enough to take me all the way to Illinois, where they lived. Daddy's tone quickly changed after we reached Illinois and made several phone calls, including one to D.O.T. to discuss an audit. That nice man & family who rescued me from the rest area got my former boss scared enough to pay me $500.00. He sent it via Western Union that same day.

We were all cheering her for getting paid and then I asked her, "How did you get back to Indiana?"

Mel lit another cigarette with her blue eyes glowing. "That same family had a relative in Indianapolis who owned a small trucking company. He agreed to interview me. They put me on a Greyhound bus in Peoria. The interview didn't pan out. They were hoping I was closer to two years' experience, so I stayed in a hotel for a few days, unsure of what to do. I kept looking at job ads, and then I saw an ad in the paper for this company and gave it a shot. To my surprise, Ron Anderson talked to me on the phone for nearly an hour, then he gave me a job. He also gave me a room at the company hotel until I can get a few paychecks and figure something out."

"That explains how that family knew how to scare that piece of crap into paying you. Your story is pretty wild. Welcome aboard, you will do great here." Carlos said with a smile. We all agreed, welcoming her. Mel answered with a heart-felt thank you.

It was time to go. Leroy tossed $5.00 on the table, and Carlos and I each tossed down another $5.00. The server deserved a decent tip; we tied up her table for over two hours, and she was very sweet about it. Leroy and I gave Carlos an additional $10 bucks each to help pay the food and drink bill. Carlos thanked us, and before we left, we made sure Mel had our phone numbers.

~ ~

Chapter Ten

Ron's Birthday Party & Random Stories

Several good things happened. Brian quit shortly after Ron put the fear of God into him. Larry had been wanting days, so that worked out. After Ron had attended the corporate meeting, Harold was let go. Ron hired an actual safety man named Timothy. He did his job well and commented shortly after he hired on that we never actually had a safety department. It took him a while to sort everything out and set it up. It didn't take long before we were all rounded up to take a physical exam. Drug and alcohol testing was still a few years away.

On a hot Saturday in July, we threw a birthday party for Ron. Eleanor brought the cake. Lisa, along with a few of us, decorated the driver's room. A grill was set up by the new night dispatcher for burgers and hot dogs. His name was Andy, an all-around great guy. He claimed he was a chef in a past life. Cooking was his passion, but didn't quite pay the bills. Andy always had a kind word, and we felt fortunate to have him as our new night dispatcher.

All the drivers who could come brought something. Whether it was a bag of chips or a pack of sodas, it was appreciated. Roger showed up with his sister and a huge Tupperware bowl of potato salad. His sister, Molly, was a sweetheart who said she loved to make food and prepared it. We made her feel welcome, and we all said the more the merrier! Carlos' wife made a big pot of baked beans. I brought plates, cups, and plastic silverware. It was a great party.

During the celebration, I handed Ron a wrapped box, which, of course, was a switchblade that was very similar to mine. I struck gold and found it at a pawnshop near Detroit. Ron was thrilled to say the least. He never stopped grinning. Men love toys no matter their age.

Mel told us later that she was upset she couldn't make it. There were a few others who were out on runs that day too. Many of us wondered if she wasn't there by design because she couldn't be trusted not to bring a keg. We'll never know.

Work and life continued. Mel rolled up her sleeves and did the job right along with the rest of us. She and I crossed paths every so often.

Shortly after the party, we were on a run together going to the East Coast. We stopped for lunch at a truck stop in the middle of Pennsylvania. We both noticed the hotel next door but gave it little thought, it's not that uncommon. We found a table that suited us and ordered our food.

Things got strange when a regular-looking guy started walking laps around our table. He was assessing both of us, which was both annoying and hilarious.

He finally stopped in front of Mel and said, "I choose you."

Mel leaned back in her seat. "Excuse me? What are you mumbling about? I don't speak bullshit."

The guy stammered, "Well if you're priced right, then we can have a good time. May I take you to the hotel next door?"

Mel lit a cigarette. With her perfect resting bitch face, she said, "How dare you strut around our table and act like an entitled moron. Stop interrupting our lunch."

Just for effect, I reached for my switchblade. "We are professional drivers, and you have five seconds to disappear."

I swear he made a new land speed record leaving our table. Mel and I laughed until our sides hurt.

Our food came, and she told me a great story detailing one of her first runs for us:

"Brian sent me to a warehouse in Columbus, Ohio that ordered some junk boxed up on pallets. I arrived and got backed in ok. No problem. I got the paperwork in order and handed it over to the receiver. After that, I needed to pee. I mean, my eyeballs were floating. I politely asked the receiver if there was a ladies' room, and he directed me to the office. He said he stays out of the Lion's Den, and I could only imagine what he meant by that. I went inside the office and saw three women busy with stuff. One of them was standing up next to a filing cabinet and the other two were at their desks, completely ignoring me. I asked the ladies if I could use the restroom. It was near where I was standing. They continued to ignore me. The one standing up barely turned around and gave me a dirty look. A look that could kill you kind of look. None of them were speaking to me or to each other. The place had a hostile feel and a second later one of them who was sitting down at her desk reached over and picked up her big, heavy oversized purse. She lifted it up for just a second, then dropped it hard onto the floor, all while giving me the death glare."

"This is going to get good, isn't it?" I remarked.

"That was my cue to leave their private little office space so the heck with being polite, I just helped myself to their cozy ladies' room, but of course, this isn't the end of the story. I was just sitting there on the potty an extra minute when one of the three cranks came walking into the bathroom. There were three stalls, and I was using the one at the far end. It only took a minute before the silly bitch realized someone else was in the bathroom. She asked, 'Is that you, Mary?' Right in the middle of taking a pee herself. I couldn't resist, so I answered her in a deep growly voice, 'No, I am a homeless stranger. I just walked in and helped myself.' This woman was so dumb; she had no clue that I just asked to use the bathroom not even five minutes ago."

Mel can barely hold her composure while telling me this story.

"So, this dumb bitch screamed, 'SECURITY!!! HELP!!!' I peeked around the stall door to watch her panic as she continued to yell and scream. She was fastening her pants while running out of the bathroom. Tears were streaming down my face from laughing so hard. I composed myself, washed my hands, and calmly left the bathroom. The three women are in a full on panic, making frantic calls, and causing a big scene. I quietly walked out without them noticing me."

"Wow Mel, that's a great story. Those women were just rude."

"Yes, absolutely rude and mean, with a lot of dumb sprinkled in."

"When I got back out to the docks, the receiver told me I had made a pretty big ruckus with the office women."

His phone was ringing steadily with hysterical women on the other end. He laughed and said, "You made my day a lot harder, but those women are mean to everyone, and they certainly deserved whatever you did."

"I smiled big and nodded. He handed me the signed bill for the load, and I was quickly out of there after that."

"Wow, we encounter all different people for sure," I said, then shifted in my chair.

"I have to tell you about the time I literally had to wrestle a guy off of me in Chicago."

"Can't wait to hear this," Mel said, grinning.

"Just after our pizza with Carlos, Brian sent me to the north side of Chicago to pick up a load of ground plastic pellets going to a customer in Atlanta. It was an 800-mile run. I left early enough to have plenty of time for all of my rest breaks and be legal. The customer wanted the plastic delivered early Wednesday morning. I had more than enough time. My load time was 9 am Monday morning. I could make the pick-up with plenty of time to spare. After getting lost three times in Chicago trying to find streets that didn't have a low bridge, I arrived. This customer had an enclosed dock off of a side street. Those are miserable. You can't see anything."

"Oh yeah, I hate those. I learned to put a flashlight on the dock bumper to illuminate where I need to back up. You absolutely can't see crap," Mel said.

"I know, right?" I said, agreeing.

"There was barely enough light, but I got backed in alright. I noticed the area was cluttered with junked up pallets and machine parts haphazardly strewn all over. I had to be careful. The lights weren't switched on until the receiver came out to load me. This guy was maybe a year or two younger than me, definitely a skinny little piss ant. He had light brown hair and crooked teeth and he bugged me to no end."

Mel sits straighter in her seat in anticipation.

"He blurts out, I ain't never seen a girl driver before. I introduced myself from my driver's seat with my window rolled down. Instead of loading me, he runs back up to my window every few minutes to ask me more questions. I tried rolling my window up and just ignoring him, but he just taps... tap... tap... tap... until I would roll it back down and talk to him."

"You are the prettiest thing I've ever seen." On and on.

"He slowly loads me but just one or two pallets at a time, then he comes running back up to my window again. I am getting pissed at this point and ask, 'Can you please just get me loaded? I have a long way to drive.' He doesn't stop bugging me."

"He sounds like a nightmare," Mel said, still grinning.

"He was, and then he gets himself all worked up."

This guy won't stop. "Hey, I just was wondering if you ever date receivers?"

"Nope, can you please get me loaded soon?"

I feel the forklift go in and out of the truck a couple more times. He only had to put 20 pallets on my truck, and it's already been an hour. He only had ten more pallets to go, and my time to get to Atlanta was shrinking away.

I closed my window and sat in my bunk, out of his sight, hoping he would get me finished up. Not a chance as he comes trotting back up to my truck. Tap...tap...tap... until I sat back down in the driver's seat and rolled down my window again.

"What do you want now?" I said, completely pissed.

"Hey, I just wanted to know if you were married or not...you know...um... just wondering 'bout that."

"Look, I am just trying to get you to load my truck so I can leave. I don't know what to say or do to make you do your job. So please do your job!"

Mel squealed with excitement, "I know this is going to get really good!"

This guy must like angry women because he must have heard: 'my life will end right this second if you don't have sex with me.'

"At that moment, he flung open my door and pushed himself directly onto my lap. To make matters worse, he took a big handful of my right breast and tried to plant a slobbery kiss on me. Big mistake. My reflexes are fast. Before he could take another breath, I shoved him off my lap, which put him off balance. He was half-way out of my truck at this point when my fist slammed hard into his nose. He went flying backwards out of my open truck door, missing the steps completely. His body crashed onto a loose pallet of assorted machine parts sitting on the concrete floor next to where my truck was. I saw blood spurting out from his nose as he quickly scrambled through a door leading inside to the offices."

"Are you effing kidding me?" Mel said. "I would have loved to have seen the carnage. He deserved that. It amazes me how many guys out here think women drivers are easy."

"That's the problem we face, Mel. Women aren't supposed to be professional drivers. So that means we are going to be targets until the industry catches up. It will take decades."

"I can't disagree," Mel said.

"I knew I was in big trouble, so I climbed out of my truck and sat on the edge of my catwalk. I fit perfectly in that area between the tractor and trailer. About two or three minutes later, a really pissed off man came barreling through that same door into the dock area.

"Who the hell do you think you are?? You busted the face of my receiver! What the hell is going on!!???"

He was standing about five feet away with his arms crossed. He forcefully screamed that part. I kept my cool and stayed put on my catwalk.

"Well, for starters, Mr. Supervisor, I have been here for well over an hour. All your receiver had to do was load 20 pallets on my truck. The pallets were already staged and ready, so all he had to do was push them on my trailer. He wouldn't stop making comments and getting up in my face about dating him."

The face on that receiver changed from furious to perplexed. He took a step back.

"Er, ma'am, can you explain?"

"Sure, I asked your guy to kindly get me loaded because I have a long way to drive. He ignored me and kept on asking me questions about my marital status and throwing out comments about me being pretty and how he wanted to date me and crap like that."

"Well, miss trucker lady, do you realize you broke his nose? He is on his way to the hospital thanks to my secretary, who was kind enough to drive him. What do you have to say about that?" I stayed perfectly calm. "Your receiver was feeling brave when he flung open my truck door, climbed onto my lap, and grabbed a handful of my right breast. Then tried to kiss me, which was gross and uncalled for. My temper got the best of me because I didn't appreciate being mauled by your receiver."

His anger turned to panic. "What? He did THAT? Ok...ok...ok...no need to get upset here. How about I get you loaded really fast, and we will just forget this just happened?"

"I will accept that. It's just upsetting because I could have already been an hour down the road if mister randy pants receiver would have just done his job."

"Wow, just wow. I would have done the same thing, maybe even jumped down and busted two or three of his ribs, too." Mel said.

"Ooooh, you're brutal, Mel. Anyway, the supervisor jumped on the forklift, and I was loaded and out of there in fifteen minutes. I never once offered an apology for busting his nose. I made it down to Atlanta in time to get a decent night's sleep."

"Do you have more stories?" Mel asked.

"Sure, I could tell you about Chief Sparkle Feather."

"Oh, please do!" Mel said, already snickering. She lit another cigarette in anticipation.

"This goes back to one of my first runs. My CB radio wasn't hooked up yet. Brian dispatched me to a food warehouse near Carlisle, PA, with a load of canned goods. A truck passed me shortly after getting on the Pennsylvania Turnpike with hardly any other late afternoon traffic in sight. No big deal and a gazillion trucks have passed by me so far except this driver got a good look at me and he decided he wanted to talk on the CB radio. He slowed his big fancy shiny chromed out truck down to a crawl and forced me to pass him."

"There are some gorgeous trucks out here," Mel said.

"For sure. So, my not so fancy, simple Freightliner cabover glided past him in the left lane. He frantically waved his microphone at me, grinning out of his window as I passed by. I couldn't answer him since my radio was still in the box. He quickly sped up to pass me back. He drove up right beside me in the left lane and looked straight at me, talking and laughing into his mike.

This guy thinks I can hear him, and we are playing a cat-and-mouse game. He doesn't realize he is talking to himself right into thin air. We passed each other back and forth for about ten miles at 60 mph. Finally, I had enough of this guy and pulled over onto the shoulder. Of course, he stopped too, easing his big fancy, shiny, chromed out truck onto the shoulder of the highway right behind me."

Mel is hanging on every word.

"I sat still and watched him from my mirror. In a quick minute, a tall man wearing a cowboy hat with a huge plume of colorful feathers sticking out of it, pretty cowboy boots, and a huge grin on his face walked up to my driver's side door. This guy could have been a bad actor from a spaghetti western. Call him Chief Sparkle Feather.

"Whatcha doin' with yer clothes still on?"

He was searching for my door handle to let himself in my truck. I had my door locked tight and the window down only partway, and I completely ignored his comment.

"May I help you with something?" I was stone faced, pretending none of this just happened.

That big grin washed off his face in a quick hurry when he asked, "Huh? What? Whaaatttt? You didn't hear anything I said?"

"Nope," I said, then held up the unopened box containing my radio.

"My radio isn't hooked up yet. I don't even have antennas mounted on my truck."

His instant embarrassment was hilarious. Chief Sparkle Feather quickly walked back to his truck. It only took a moment for him to pull back onto the highway and put the hammer down. I laughed so hard.

"Chief sparkle feather ha ha ha ha!! I am set for the rest of the day!" Mel said, in hysterics.

We wrapped up our lunch and then finished our runs to New Jersey. We tried talking on the CB while heading across eastern PA, but the other drivers were constantly hurling jabs and insults at us. We were split up after our deliveries. She had a pickup in Harrisburg, and I went down to Baltimore for my backhaul. I was excited to be going to Baltimore because the harbor tunnel was the coolest thing ever. Actually, all the bridge and tunnel systems on the East Coast are all pretty amazing feats of engineering.

~ ~

Chapter Eleven

Yankers

This section is dedicated to all the knuckleheads that thought pulling up beside us in their cars and believing that exposing themselves would somehow convince us to pull over and service them. I promise you, this was never the outcome. This happened a lot. Cell phones and cameras weren't a thing yet. These men did nothing but harass us and occasionally create fear, making us believe they might intentionally ram into us to make us stop.

One story comes to mind for exactly this. I was in Michigan, heading north on Highway 23. My destination was Plymouth with a load of something or other, and I was about twenty minutes south of highway 14 where I would exit off. I was being passed by a car when the driver realized I was female. He slowed down next to me and matched my speed. This guy immediately exposed himself and began playing with his junk. This idiot became adamant about me pulling off every exit that had a hotel by honking, pointing, and being obnoxious. He swerved into my lane a few times to get my attention. I was ignoring him to the best of my ability and really wondered if he was going to hit me to force me onto the shoulder. This went on and on until finally, traffic picked up, and he had to pay more attention to driving. My exit was coming up in a couple of miles. I gradually slowed down; traffic was piling up behind him, so he had to pass me. I safely took the exit and was never so glad to be away from someone.

*****

Another time I was near Louisville, Kentucky. It was morning. I was at a stoplight, getting ready to exit onto Highway 64. To my right, at the stoplight, was a nice-looking man in a suit, probably heading to the office or wherever. We made eye contact, so I smiled at him and said, "Good morning." Of course, he couldn't hear me, but he understood and returned a quick good morning and wave. Well, that should have been it, right? Nope, that guy chased me for a few miles, getting too close and pointing to his exposed dick in anticipation. Why, just why? That guy went from a hero to a zero in a millisecond. Eventually, he gave up and disappeared into traffic.

*****

Melanie, being a blue-eyed blonde, had even more trouble. One day we were hanging out at the yard and this topic came up. We talked about how pushy these guys can be.

Mel said, "I was just motoring down the highway listening to some great rock music and minding my own business when this car showed up and, of course, he hung out next to me. He pulled his junk out and stayed next to me for quite a distance. He got so demanding at one point he crowded into my lane, nearly forcing me into the dirt. I thought about just pulling over and beating him to death with my tire club. That would be justifiable homicide. Right?"

"It should be! How did you escape him?" I asked.

"I took a chance and flew off an unplanned exit, nearly toppling over, but that was just about my only option other than flattening his head. He was in the left lane and couldn't exit quickly enough to keep up with me. I pulled onto the shoulder after taking that exit and sat still for a few minutes. The road was wide enough that I easily made a U-turn and got right back onto the highway when I felt ready. These idiots pop up out of nowhere and we can't shake them off."

"It's the curse of being female and trying to do our jobs," I said.

Mel continued, "Not long after I hired on, I had a run to upstate New York. About halfway there, I needed fuel, which was part of the job, of course. The truck stop wasn't too busy. I fueled and parked, trying to decide if I wanted a shower after eating. My time was a bit tight, so I opted to just go in and grab a burger. As soon as I locked my truck door, I heard someone shouting, "Hey blondie, get over here! It's my turn!"

"What the heck? I just ignored him and headed toward the building. Next thing I knew, there was a hard yank of my hair, and I went halfway down to the ground. He was trying to drag me. I was instantly in fighting mode, so it's on! I came up kicking, cursing, and swinging. My fist connected to his right eye, and he reeled back, howling. A couple of drivers quickly came to my rescue and pulled this guy off of me. There was yelling, and the cops were called, but this chicken shit loser ran back to his truck and took off like a bat out of hell. Hopefully, he had a black eye for days."

******

Several months passed before I met up with Mel again. She had left a message on my answering machine to meet her at T 5 on a Saturday night in January. T 5 was the old exit number for the turnpike at Toledo. Exit 5 was the last exit for Toledo, heading east. This exit put you on I-280. There was a Truckstop of America off of the exit and a busy trucker bar north of that. She was heading back from the east coast and figured I would head east. I was under a load going to Albany, New York, but I didn't have to leave until Sunday. I debated a long time if I wanted to spend my Saturday night at a bar. The weather was nasty, with snow coming down at a pretty good clip. I was a little more than sideways about this idea, but in the end, I decided to go. I dug through my freezer, found a pot pie, and tossed it in the oven. After eating, I packed my bags, then slid on my usual jeans, a flannel shirt and, of course, my leg warmers. Whoever invented leg warmers deserved a hug. Cowboy boots were never my style. I wore regular work boots instead.

At 5 pm, the yard was covered with several inches of snow and deserted. While my truck was warming up, I brushed the snow off of the windows, then I went inside to grab the paperwork for the load. It was paper products loaded on a dry van. At least I didn't have to babysit a reefer. I started my logbook and run sheet. Things went downhill after that because I jumped my pin while trying to hook up. This happens when the trailer is dropped too high. It's a royal pain to crank the loaded trailer a couple of inches higher so you can pull your tractor out from underneath. The edge of the fifth wheel usually gets caught behind the trailer pin. It's hard to explain. I managed to get my tractor unstuck and back on track. I cranked the trailer down, then hooked it up properly.

The drive to Toledo took nearly three hours due to the winter storm. The roads were quite nasty with so much snow and ice accumulating. It was 8 pm when I got there and luckily found a spot in the back, away from the building.

The bar was surprisingly busy. I left my truck running because I didn't need it to freeze solid.

Country music was blaring loud enough to hear outside. I walked into a blue haze of smoke, and Ricky Skaggs music. Many people were dancing and partying wearing fringed vests, cowboy boots and hats.

Mel saw me and came trotting over. She gave me a big hug and showed me to her table. A server came over and I ordered a tequila and orange juice. "Ok got it, a tequila sunrise." She said.

"Not quite," I said. "No grenadine please."

"Okay, got it."

"Wow," Mel said. "I expected you to be boring and just order a coffee."

"I can have a bit of fun. Besides, I will sleep here tonight. That storm is getting worse."

"Storm?" Mel asked, raising an eyebrow.

"Never mind." I said, figuring she has drank too much already. Pretty soon, Reba McIntire was singing about whoever was in New England. Mel was quickly scooped up by a handsome guy and off they went to dance. I sat back and watched everyone. A few songs later, two couples approached my table and asked me if I was Mel's friend. "Yes, we work for the same company." I smiled politely and asked why they were interested.

"Oh, she is a regular here. She talks about the people she knows. We were just curious."

The song was over and Mel, along with her handsome guy, joined up with all of us. Mel was animated. She was in her comfort zone, surrounded by beer and friends. Soon an empty pitcher was picked up and a full one replaced it.

"Remember a while back when we were talking about yankers?" Mel asked.

"Yes, why?"

"Well, shortly after that meet up, wouldn't you just know it? I was heading west to Kansas City when I found myself in a battle for my lane with a very pushy yanker. This idiot was determined to have me service him. He made several attempts to get me to pull over. I refused, and he got frustrated. Then he jammed his right fender directly into my left steps. He was trying his best to shove me onto the shoulder. I wasn't having it and became one big fur ball of pissed off, angry female. I accelerated hard and shot directly into the left lane with him still against my steps, and forcefully pushed him straight into the ditch on the far side. After that, the only thing visible was the ass end of his car sticking up and a plume of dirt. My deed was done, and I was gone in a flash."

We all clapped, hooted and hollered, praising Mel for taking control and literally ditching this guy.

"I got one better," said a woman in the group whom we all had just met.

"My husband and I are a team. Anyway, he was sick and took a week off. I don't mind running the truck without him once in a while. We also have a retired police dog named Sarge who always rides with us. Sarge is smarter than the average person. He knows commands perfectly. So yes, pretty much the same story. I was heading east on highway 44 from Springfield, Missouri, on schedule to make a pickup in St. Louis later that same day. To my annoyance, I had a persistent yanker who wouldn't take a hint. Sarge noticed my unease and was stuck to my side. After several miles of this jackass in my face with his junk, I told Sarge to stay low. Then, I gave the yanker the thumbs up. We took the next exit that had a motel and, fortunately, a large rear parking lot. He was beyond thrilled to exit off with me. I parked way off in the far corner of this big empty lot. He parked next to me, then he got out all set to have some fun. I opened my truck door and got out. This late thirty something average man was looking at me, kind of wondering what the delay was. I smiled sweetly and asked him if he was ready for some fun.

He said, let's go! I said, absolutely, and hollered for Sarge. Next thing, this guy was being stared down by a huge, snarling German shepherd with big, raised hackles. This guy couldn't run away fast enough. I gave the order to injure. Sarge immediately jumped on this guy and sunk his teeth deep into his shoulder, tearing him up. After a lot of injury, I hollered at Sarge to stop. He immediately did, leaving this guy on the ground screaming in pain. Then, Sarge looked at me, asking for something. I nodded and Sarge took a piss close enough to splash him, then he finished up by taking a big dump right by his head. I told the guy that was great fun. Sarge and I got back up in the truck and, of course, I patted his head and gave him two treats. We headed off and enjoyed the rest of our day."

Her husband stayed quiet and grinned while she told the story, then he said this was his favorite story and how proud he was of her standing up for herself and how proud he was of Sarge too. He gave her a big hug and kiss while the rest of us were rendered speechless. There were no words. We all felt uncomfortable and just let her story slide past.

Mel was having the time of her life, and I was glad that I joined her. It was coming up on midnight when I said good night to everyone and headed back out to my truck. Mel and her handsome guy said they were going to get a room.

I walked out into the storm and noticed that a few more inches of snow had fallen. My truck was warm, and I was beyond ready for a good night's sleep. I peeled my cigarette stench clothes off and went to bed. Before I drifted off, I thought about that woman's story and decided that she didn't have to deal with him that harshly. Sure, some things are deserved, but sometimes there are better ways of handling things. I strongly felt that she went too far.

By morning, the storm was over. I drove down to the nearby truck stop and treated myself to a shower then I ordered breakfast. It was noon before I decided to head out making sure the plows had enough time to clear the snow from the turnpike and the N.Y. thruway. The rest of my trip was uneventful.

~ ~

Chapter Twelve

Bad Guys

This next story is about a plant manager who let his title and authority go to his head. The typical arrogant bully of a human being whose only job was to make everyone's life miserable. This happened in the late 1980s. My dispatch was to pick up a load of freshly boxed meat at a large meat packing plant in eastern Nebraska and deliver it asap to a cold storage in New England. I showed up on time for a 7 am appointment. It took anywhere from three hours to all day to get loaded, depending on how fast the meat gets packaged. Sometimes, it's already packaged and ready to load.

I badly needed a shower and was well aware that the changing rooms for men and women in these places had showers. All I needed was permission. So far, so good. I got my dock assignment and backed in.

The loader greeted me on the dock. He was a friendly, large black man. He said my load time would be within the three-hour window. I felt comfortable enough to ask him if I could use the women's locker room to shower.

"You must get permission from the plant manager." Answered the loader.

"Where can I find him?"

"Hard to say, but please tread carefully around that man."

I looked at the loader, and we locked eyes. Nothing else needed to be said.

A second or two later, there was a commotion as a cocky man wearing jeans and a dress shirt approached the dock. While introducing himself, he gave me a thorough once-over, as if I was there solely for his entertainment.

"It's nice to make your acquaintance." His name was Kevin, and he stood there, momentarily lost for words.

"So why are you standing on my dock?"

"I am here to pick up a load for New England."

"Oh, well then. Interesting. I think you are the first woman driver I have seen in ages."

"That's great," I said, somewhat annoyed. "May I ask you a favor? May I please use the shower in the ladies' locker room?"

Kevin grinned in a cringe way and said, "I can give you permission, but first, I would love to show you around the plant."

Oh, great, I was thinking. All I wanted to do was clean up, and this was going to be a circus. I had no idea what was coming. Kevin was slow walking me to each area and describing what each work station did. I didn't need to know. The part that made this hard was him showing off by lashing out at workers just because he could. Kevin was especially obnoxious with the female workers. For example, if they weren't standing up straight enough or hair nets weren't to his liking. He even told one, "You know, your red hair means you aren't your daddy's daughter." She was used to the torment and completely ignored him. This was clearly the case everywhere we went; the women brilliantly didn't respond. Kevin did his best to intimidate but was only ignored. He tried anything and everything he could find to bully and torment. It was painful to watch. If he wasn't yelling, he was ogling, looking at the women like they were prey. The men, same as the women, didn't flinch or pay him any mind. Interestingly enough, their faces conveyed absolute hatred and disgust. I tried to hurry this along, but it fell on deaf ears.

"Let's go have some fun," he said while opening the door to a stairway. My heart sank as he handed me a white hard hat and a white lab coat that was hanging on a hook nearby. He insisted I wear that stuff, and then we went upstairs to a viewing platform.

My heart sank. Below us on the floor were a line of tables and workers doing a process of some sort. It looked like they were injecting chicken or pork. It was hard to see from that high up.

The "fun" was intimidation. We were essentially lording over ten workers, two of whom were female. One woman was young and a nervous wreck, and I could only assume she was new.

She was very close to tears while being watched. She looked up at me, distressed. I flashed her a great big smile and gave her two thumbs up.

This was it for me. I was beyond angry at Kevin at that point. I made my way to the staircase, removed my hat and coat, and abruptly stated, "I just wanted to take a shower. This is pure meanness."

"Hold up, we can get you the shower. I just wanted to show you around my domain." Kevin actually said that. I wanted to choke him. He was chasing me back to the docks, hollering at me to hang on for a second.

"I have seen enough," I said, pissed.

"Follow me to my office, then I will tell you where you can find the locker rooms."

Lord, help me, I thought. "Okay fine."

He walked me all the way back through the plant to a nearly hidden corner office. He went in first and sat at his desk. I didn't go past the doorway despite his begging. I wasn't trusting him not to lock the door behind me. Kevin got a big crap eating grin on his face. He leaned back in his chair, then he put his feet up on the desk in a 'come get me' pose. The entitlement of this guy was beyond scary and way out of line.

"As soon as you get showered and prettied up, come right back here and see me. The locker rooms are near the docks. Just ask the loader."

He just gave me an out, so I played along. "That sounds like a great idea Kevin, I think we would have a great time! Just wait right here. I will be back in a jiffy."

I smiled, but deep down, I just wanted to leave as fast as I could. To say Kevin was a predator is an understatement. I ran back to the docks. The loader had a concerned look.

"I was wondering if we were ever going to see you again."

"No kidding. That guy is a piece of work."

"He is mean to the ladies. Really mean, you don't know how rotten he really is." The loader said.

"So sorry you all have to deal with him. Why hasn't anyone put in a complaint?" I asked.

"Several have tried, but the backlash is so severe we're all just better off taking the abuse. Anyway, your truck will be done in about 30 minutes. It went quickly today. The locker room is right over there. Get your shower done as fast as possible and meet me right back here. Your paperwork will be ready."

I did just that. I grabbed my bags and a change of clothes. The shower was great. I looked around for a hidden camera. I wouldn't have put it past Kevin to pull a stunt like that. When I returned to the dock, the loader was just sliding the last pallet on. He had me sign the paperwork.

"Hurry and pull away from the dock. I will close your doors and put the seal on. Leave like a phantom jet."

The loader was a godsend. It must have been divine intervention that I never had to pick up a load there again. Bonus - I made it to New England 24 hours later, and the manager of the cold storage gave me a 100 dollar bill for getting there so fast. Score!

******

A few years later, I was being chased by three other truckers who decided they were going to act really stupid. I was loaded with pallets of expensive praline candy that I had picked up in Louisiana the previous day. My CB radio was on, but I hadn't been talking to anyone, just the occasional voices in the background as drivers chatted with each other. Conversations were fading in and out. I was driving through Tennessee, heading north to the yard with my reefer set on cool, minding my own business when, out of the clear blue, I heard the squawk of a driver keying up. "Breaker - breaker one nine - this is the Widow Maker, and I am heading southbound. Did I just see a northbound female pulling a freezer box?"

"Not sure, Widow Maker this here is Gator Breath, and maybe I can get a look at it."

These bonehead drivers are looking for trouble. I am not saying a word.

Screeeeeech from another driver keying up, "Hey boys, count me in, this is the Chicken Tamer, and I think I see the ass-end of her freezer box. Maybe we can catch up to that hot beaver and get us a piece."

Okay, they are somewhere behind me. My hackles are up now.

"Breaker - breaker one nine - this is Hog Wild back here somewhere and did I hear we got us a bearded taco up ahead?"

"Yea, this is Widow Maker, and I said hot beaver, not bearded taco, you dumb ass. Hey boys, Widow Maker continued, I am gonna miss out on all this fun 'cause by the time I get turned back around, y'all would be havin' yer beaver steak.

Squuuaaakkk from Hog Wild because his radio is making a fuss. "Sorry 'bout your luck, Widow maker. I am pulling up the rear back here somewhere, so let's go get her. Does anyone have a twenty on her location?"

"This is Chicken Tamer, and I think I am leading you boys, and best I can tell, our beaver meat is only a mile ahead of us. You boys got some zip under yer hoods?" The other two quickly keyed up and said, "Yep."

These three boys were chasing me. Chicken Tamer was closing in behind me with Gator Breath behind him and Hog Wild pulling up the rear. I am listening to all this while enjoying the beautiful day, not worried yet about my pursuers. Not saying a word.

"This is Gator Breath, and I need you to slow up a bit so I can be right behind you when we get her."

"Same back here," hollered Hog Wild through a squawking microphone.

"Okay, you boys put some pedal to the metal. I will slow up, then we will round us up a beaver."

"Hey, this is Gator Breath. Have any of you boys figured out just how we're gonna capture us this hot little beaver?"

"Yea," said Chicken Tamer, "What I am fixin' to do is pass her, then get right smack in front of her and slow her down to keep her from slipping out of our grip. I need you, Gator Breath, to get right next to her in the left lane so she can't escape us boys. Hog Wild can be tight on her ass and keep her from getting away."

I am listening to all this, and they don't realize I am hearing their ridiculous plan. It sounds like they are planning on forcing me to stop and then all three, gang raping me. On the side of the road, really? Can't wait to see how this works out for them.

Their plan was in place, and not another sound was coming through the radio. In fact, it was completely and eerily silent for a while since those boys started up this noise. Not a single breaker 1-9 from another trucker; this struck me as telling, considering there was plenty of noise before these three boys started up. Nearby drivers listen instead of talking. I don't have any worries at this point other than one of those numbskulls causing a massive wreck.

The best part of this crazy plan is they have no clue what I even look like, and all this started from a trucker heading south in the opposite direction who couldn't have possibly seen anything except that I was a girl. This is so funny to me; I could be Broom Hilda for all they knew. I could see them in my mirrors. They were closing in fast.

"Hey boys, this is Hog Wild back here in line, and we are just about on her tail. I am closing the gap and have just one quick question for you two?... ummm... are you boys sure this is the right thing to do? I mean, you are talking about trapping a female driver and then literally raping her, right? I mean, this could turn out kinda bad for us. I never hurt a woman in my life, and I am definitely not a rapist."

"Yupper, said Chicken Tamer, You in or ain't ya? Ya know any woman drivin a truck is looking to get laid. We are just gonna take what's already ours; we're just gonna have a little harmless fun."

"This is Chicken Tamer in the lead, and I am close enough to lick the numbers off the back of her reefer. Okay boys, I'm gettin' ready to pass her and slow her down. I ain't been home in three weeks and I'm horny as a three peckered Billy goat."

"I am ready too," chimed in Gator Breath, who was instructed to get next to me in the left lane. We are all running about 65 mph. According to these boys, I am to be pushed off onto the shoulder, trapped and raped. We'll see about that.

Three big shiny trucks in a row are closing in behind me. I am watching them in my mirror. Chicken Tamer pulled into the left lane, aligning himself to pass me and then to position himself in front to slow me down. I waited until he was midway into his pass, almost next to me, and without allowing him to get a look. I have my left arm up to block his view.

I can't let him pass yet. I need Gator Breath in the left lane right behind Chicken Tamer; I need them both right next to me, so I speed up to 68 mph.

Chicken Tamer keys up, "Hurry up Gator Breath and get behind me!"

I am watching as Gator Breath eases into the left lane, right behind Chicken Tamer. Perfect.

Hog Wild is now right on my rear, exactly where I need him to be. All three trucks are positioned exactly where I need them to be.

Right now, and fast! I turned on my four-way flashers, then immediately and forcefully slammed on my brakes hard enough to smoke them, locking them up and giving off a huge grayish blue blast of smoke. I go into a hellacious skid, laying about 50 yards of black rubber marks on the highway. This maneuver forced all three trucks to pass me by like jets.

Zooooooooom goes Chicken Tamer.

Zooooooooom goes Gator Breath.

Zoooooooooom goes Hog Wild, who was forced to pass me immediately or crash instantly to his death into the rear of my trailer. He cursed loudly and yelled out on his CB radio, half- panicked, "God damned female nearly killed me back here!"

They were going fast enough that now they are pretty far ahead trying to figure out what just happened.

"Hey, this is Gator Breath, and what in the sam hill just happened back there?"

"I think we just messed this whole thing up. Did any of you get a look at her?"

Chicken Tamer keyed up, "Boys, I think we just got outsmarted by our little beaver. I reckon she heard us talking."

"I sure wanted that beaver."

"Me too, partner," said the other two, talking over each other. I let out a huge sigh of relief, my heart pounding with relief as all three boys zoomed past me with no choice.

After nearly coming to a stop in the right lane of the highway, I sped up, then realized there was an exit ramp ahead in about a half mile. It connected to a decent secondary highway. There was a little fuel stop on the right. I took the exit to decompress. Fortunately, those boys were already way past. While parking my truck, I thought about how dangerously close we all came to getting seriously injured. One of them could have easily lost control trying to push me onto the shoulder and caused a massive pileup.

A Tennessee state trooper pulled off the exit right behind me and parked next to me. He quickly got out of his car and stepped over to my truck door.

"Please step out of your truck, ma'am." I got out really fast, wondering what I had just done. "I saw you being chased down by three male drivers. I need to assess that you are alright."

"Yes, sir, that was me."

"Are you okay, ma'am?"

"Yes, thank you for asking, officer. I am fine."

"Your maneuver was brilliant. I was closing in on the truck directly behind you and saw the entire thing."

"Did you hear them talking?" I asked the Officer, already knowing the answer was yes.

"Yes, in fact, I was heading the other direction and made a flip. I was listening and closing in at the same time. I also called in some help, ma'am. You were not going to be harmed, not on my watch."

"Thank you, Officer, for responding to all that nonsense."

He spoke with authority. "Those boys are in for a surprise. I radioed ahead when I saw all this taking place. We're setting up portable scales in the rest area a few miles up the road. Four troopers have already caught up to them. These boys will be escorted into the rest area and detained for a while. Stay on this secondary road until the next town. There will be an exit that will merge you back onto the highway."

"Thank you so very much. I appreciate your response and professionalism."

"Have a good rest of your day, ma'am, and drive safe."

"Thank you, I will."

He sped off in a hurry as soon as he knew I was alright.

I took a moment to check my tires. They were unfortunately flat spotted, but that's a better trade off than fatalities. The stupidity of these men will stay with me for a long time. The state police were nearby the entire time, hearing that crazy plan. Three unsuspecting drivers got a D.O.T. inspection they won't soon forget.

A Department of Transportation inspection can be brutal. The police have the authority to search your truck, your person, and, most importantly, your logbook. Drivers can get themselves in serious trouble because some use two and three logbooks to prove being legal through deception. The police can and will put a driver out of service for a logbook and many other violations.

****

This next story happened in the early 1990s and was the only time I had to ferry the truck for a delivery. It goes like this:

I recently completed a delivery of canned food near Battle Creek, Michigan. This was a Wednesday afternoon. I pulled into a nearby truck stop and parked so I could make a call to dispatch. The payphone receiver was coated with Bril Cream. They all were. I cleaned it off by rubbing it against my leg. All my jeans had a shiny streak near the knee from repeatedly cleaning men's hair grease off of phones. It's just the way it was.

Dispatch picked up after two rings. Becky answered, sounding excited about something.

"I have an unusual load going out to Nantucket Island. We have covered this load twice now, and it's a good one. You will love it. The customer is in Lansing, Michigan, not too far from where you are. It's building supplies. Your pickup time is 3 am tomorrow morning, and you will drive it straight there for delivery that evening."

I said, "What? Am I supposed to swim there?"

Becky laughed, "No, silly, the foreman will meet you at the Hyannis port in Massachusetts. He will pay for your ticket for the ferry ride in both directions, and he is also responsible for overseeing your truck in the cargo hold. You will be on the 7 pm ferry. It's the last one of the day going to Nantucket Island. Call me when you return to the mainland on Friday. Oh, by the way, the foreman has rooms for everyone in a nice hotel right there on the island. There is no rush to get up Friday morning."

Cushy, I thought. Becky added, "The foreman buys the driver a fresh catch seafood dinner at a nice restaurant close to the pier. He shows the guys a good time. Just remember, you aren't to touch that load or assist them during the unloading process. There will be a full crew there."

"Thank you," I said, appreciating a no-touch load.

She gave me the customer details to make the pickup. It was coming up on dinner time, which allowed plenty of time to get some sleep and a shower. My pickup point was only an hour away.

I arrived early; the shipper backed me in right away and had me done by 1:45 am. He walked up to my door and waved, "You are all set, ma'am."

"Thank you," I said as I climbed out of the truck to sign the paperwork. Then, I walked around the rig to check everything and sealed the trailer. I got back into the cab and started a new day in my logbook. I eased the truck into third gear and was rolling towards I-90 east with the delivery point on my mind. I felt terrified to drive the truck on a boat. I couldn't think about anything else. There was a thick cloud cover overhead. The weather turned crappy soon after I departed. Off and on, snow and sleet made it a sloppy, cold trip. Music from the radio and the slap-slap of the wipers kept me company. My CB radio was shut off on purpose. I didn't need the extra racket.

My assignment was what it was, and I needed to stop worrying, but I didn't like it. I was trying to believe Becky about the previous loads going there, but drivers talk when their loads are unusual. Never ever have I heard of my workmates going to Nantucket. This would have been big news.

It took fifteen hours to reach Hyannis Port from Michigan with a loaded truck, which was good despite the weather. At 5 pm that same day, I arrived and parked on the busy pier at Hyannis Port, Massachusetts. The ferry was scheduled to sail at 7 pm, which left plenty of time for dinner. I was hungry, picturing a steaming lobster and shrimp combination or something equally delicious. Breakfast wasn't much, and I needed to keep my foot in it with the weather conditions. The second issue quickly arising was the cold temps. It was 31 degrees and dropping. The freezing rain-snow mix continued. The pier had a 'no idle' rule for all vehicles parked. Everyone waiting was cold and miserable. The foreman was running late. Where the heck was he? It's coming up on 6:30 pm, and it's time for the ferry to depart soon. I am starving but can't leave my rig unattended to look for dinner. My only choice is to sit still and wait. My hoodie jacket wasn't enough. I wondered if this load of building material was even going to Nantucket. Sometimes orders get messed up.

Precisely 15 minutes before the ferry is due to set sail, the foreman comes screaming onto the pier with his fancy red sports car and slides sideways, pretending to be important. The ferry was well into the process of being loaded with vehicles and people at this point. He bought two tickets, then shoved one into his pocket.

The man had no trouble finding me and walked over to my truck. I rolled down my window to talk. He didn't say hello, but he looked straight at me and said,

"A girl driver? Seriously? I got sent a stupid girl? What the freaking hell am I supposed to do with you?" His tone was vicious.

"You don't have to do anything with me except help get this truck onto the ferry."

The icy wind was blowing around his wavy brown hair. He was a slender man wearing worn-out jeans and a blue-checkered flannel shirt. He was a normal guy in his mid-thirties, with his heavy coat slung over his arm. It's a shame he had such an unpleasant disposition. That made things unnecessarily rough. I tried to make conversation.

"Do you have a name?"

He said, "Rodney," and then he left my truck in a hurry, rushing over to park his car. He got busy gabbing with a group of people surrounding him who were also boarding. Rodney was making gestures with his hands while walking and talking, looking comfortable. He seemed at home in this place. An employee of the ferry company was flagging me to pull my truck into the cargo hold. The cars inside are packed like sardines, with almost no space left for my truck.

It would have been nice if Rodney had arrived on time. This would have allowed for an easier time getting loaded onto the boat. I already knew nothing on this trip would be easy.

There were two other trucks in the cargo hold. I was being instructed to squeeze my truck into a narrow path so tight between another truck and a car that it was only pretending to be a designated parking spot. The crewman was directing me into that spot and telling me to fold my truck mirrors flat against my windows to maximize my space.

Luckily, the big mirrors are hinged to do that, but it caused a big problem with seeing where I needed to be. The spot was so tight I had to take care not to scrape the car on my driver's side. Even worse, there was a truck in the spot to my right. With great care, I very slowly crept into that spot. Tight doesn't do this justice. Crazy tight.

Once I was parked, that same man helped me out of my truck by having me step onto the hood of the car next to me on the driver's side. I couldn't open my truck door enough to squeeze myself out, so I climbed out through my side window. The crewman lifted me off the car hood and told me I did an excellent job parking.

I gave him a nervous smile and said, "Thanks."

The same crewman brought in a half dozen more cars, and the loading was complete. I worried about the added weight to the ferry with my loaded rig. The hold was crammed with vehicles. I knew zero about boats and had to trust the people who did this for a living.

We set sail to Nantucket Sound. Rodney found me walking up from the cargo hold, and he mumbled something about missing dinner. He said I could "maybe" get a cold hot dog on the ferry. There was no way I was going to give him the satisfaction of watching me, "a stupid girl," eat a cold hot dog.

Rodney trotted off so fast after our 15-second encounter that I knew he wasn't sincere about feeding me. I was happy to see him disappear. At this point, I wouldn't have accepted anything from him. Truth be told, there was no food of any kind on the ferry because it was the last one of the day. I knew there would be an opportunity for a meal, but it wouldn't be tonight, and certainly not until I got back to the mainland sometime tomorrow. I can get through this. I kept reassuring myself.

A minute or two after Rodney skittered away, I walked on deck and spotted several chairs for the passengers. I found one off by itself and apart from a group of other passengers. I sat down, threw my hood over my head, and then stayed put as the wind bit my cheeks and cut right through my jacket. The witch of November was angry tonight.

I sat still, listening to the sound of the water rushing against the side of the boat. Whoosh-whoosh. It was a song only the ship knew. The mineral smell of the ocean was unfamiliar, and the black night water looked foreboding. I sat unmoving, frozen stiff, with no interest in any conversation. The ferry ride lasted an hour, and I was thankful nobody approached me.

The bump of docking jarred me, and I glanced at my watch like it mattered. It was 8:15 pm. It didn't matter at all. We unloaded one at a time. Backing out of the cargo hold was easy after most everyone had disembarked. Rodney hollered at me to follow him to the job site as soon as I had the rig on dry ground. My mirrors snapped back to where they belonged with a gentle push.

Rodney jumped in the waiting pickup truck with his men, and we were at the construction site in just a few minutes. The crew showed me where to back the rig in at the job site to be unloaded. I had to be careful with this because I could see a lot of debris on the ground. I looked up into the sky and only saw blackness. Creepy blackness.

Rodney was impatient because I got out of the truck twice to get a visual of the mess on the ground. I had to move a few boards out of my path and make sure the area was clear. Within a few minutes, I got the truck exactly where he asked me to put it with no issues, like possibly running a nail into a tire.

Once Rodney was satisfied with my truck position at his job site, he hollered, "Get over here bitch and start unloading this truck!"

What? Now I am a bitch? Seriously? I got out of my truck and walked over to where he was standing, then politely told him that my name was Patty, not bitch, and I was instructed not to touch any part of that load by my dispatcher. Rodney had several male crew members standing there with him. His crewmen looked embarrassed. Rodney was standing way too close to me, so I took several steps back away from him.

"Do the male drivers help you unload?" He only mumbled something about "stupid female." Rodney also didn't like it when I said I was cold, starving, exhausted, and going to bed. I turned my back on him before he could answer, and without a moment's hesitation, I climbed up into my truck, locked the doors, and closed the curtains tight.

My bunk was warm. Thankfully, I could idle my engine for heat on the island. I removed my coat and boots and then remained fully clothed. I crawled under my top blanket and left the sheets untouched. Sleep came quickly.

At midnight, someone was pounding hard on my truck door. I woke up disoriented from a deep sleep. It took a few seconds to orient myself. I pulled open my curtain and saw Rodney's face plastered against my driver's side window.

"Get up, bitch, your truck is empty. It's time to go to the hotel. You have exactly one minute. I still can't believe your company sent me a god-dammed woman."

I put my boots on fast, grabbed my bags and hoodie, and climbed out of my truck.

"Your lucky day," I said with a big smile, specifically intended to bug him.

We left the truck where it was. I shut the motor off (big mistake) and locked it up. All of us piled into the pickup truck. Rodney gave me his room number in case I had a problem. I didn't have a problem, but now with his room number I had a plan, a good one, and suddenly I felt vindicated.

The hotel was only a mile away, and it was beautiful. Very nautical, with a comfortable feel. It only took a minute for Rodney to show me to my room and slap the key in my hand. Apparently, with Rodney, everything had to be warfare. In a split second, he was gone.

The room was so pretty, with lots of pictures of whaling ships and old mariners of a time long past. I loved the crisp white linens with blue accents throughout. It was so inviting, with pleasant touches all around. It was a perfect seaside hotel. My shower was glorious and washed the events of the day away. Rodney's mean comments, no dinner, and how unpleasant this trip had been so far, all washed down the drain. After my shower, the soft bed felt wonderful, and I curled up, hugging the pillow. I was feeling restless and wanted to be off the island. Shiela, my dispatcher, must have thought she was doing something special for me. She may have had my best interest at heart, but I certainly would never allow her to dispatch me on this run again. I noticed the construction project had a long way to go. I dozed off and on watching TV until exactly 5 am, then I made a call.

"Who the hell is this!?" Rodney demanded angrily, barely awake.

My voice was sickeningly sweet in his receiver. "Put me on the 6:30 am ferry."

"What the f***!?" He spat out more than a few extra expletives, much to my delight.

"Be at my door at 5:45 am." I held the receiver away from my ear, waiting to hear a few more extremely nasty expletives. I wasn't disappointed. I enjoyed upsetting Rodney. He was having none of this.

"You have a ticket on the noon ferry!" Rodney was beyond furious.

"Change it," I said with a big grin on my face, picturing him only half-awake, struggling to process my request. I enjoyed how pissed off I just made him. Fabulous! The bitch scored one.

Rodney gave in and arrived at my door precisely at 5:45 am. He looked like a trampled bear, seething with anger. We rode in silence back to my truck, but he stopped way short.

"Get out!" he roared as soon as he slammed the pickup truck into park, throwing me forward. I grabbed my bags and had to jog the short distance. I unlocked the driver's door and jumped into my truck, instantly regretting shutting it off. It started fine, but my windshield had an icy glaze from the all-night freezing drizzle. Stupid me, I didn't leave it running. I got the defrosters blowing at high speed. I didn't have enough time to warm up the truck, so the windshield started fogging up quickly from my body heat and the temperature changing inside the cabin. I grabbed a handful of paper towels and began wiping circles to see through.

Rodney took off fast. I followed him, trying to see the road as best as I could. The heavy fog layered on top of the dark morning created a problem. His bright taillights, which illuminated the surroundings, helped me see the road and navigate. Rodney would have shut them off had he known anything under his control was helping.

It was a short drive to the pier. I parked my truck close to the nearly empty loading ramp to wait for my turn. It was 6:10 am. Rodney drove the pickup about three steps from the ticket office. He bought my ticket, then he drove over to where I parked. He shoved the ticket in my hand through my open window and cursed me one last time.

I flashed him a big smile and said, "Thanks." He didn't upset me one bit, I was over it. He turned away, slid back into the pickup, and zoomed out of my sight forever. I let out a long, drawn-out sigh of relief.

My decision to be on the 6:30 am ferry was smart. There were only a handful of passengers, which meant lots of room in the cargo hold. It was a simple task to park in there for the return trip, and I didn't have to fold in my mirrors since I was one of the very few vehicles in the hold. After getting parked in cargo, I found my way up on deck and sat down with about a dozen local travelers.

The cheerful captain declared it was 32 degrees, but at least the wind had died down, which made being on the deck tolerable. Everyone on board was pleasant. A few locals chatted with me about nothing in particular. Some passengers pointed out that it's the off-season for tourists. This time on the ferry, everything felt right.

Just after we pushed off the pier and set sail into Nantucket Sound, a gentle older woman approached us carrying a pan filled with warm, fresh-baked cinnamon rolls. The rolls were dripping with mouthwatering icing and goo, smelling so wonderful. We couldn't wait to grab a paper plate and fork and dig into them. I bought two and savored every warm bite. The woman beamed with pride. She sold the entire pan to the few of us. What a brilliant entrepreneur. The ferry had fresh hot coffee, warming our throats and helping to wash down the treat. It filled my empty stomach and tasted better than anything I had eaten in a long time. All of us gathered together, enjoying the early morning. None of us gave a rip about the cold or the morning fog hanging so low over the water that we couldn't see the far end of the ferry. Not one of us cared about anything for that hour we sailed. We talked about everything and nothing and laughed at the weird curve balls life throws at us.

At 7:30 am sharp, we docked at Hyannis Port. I easily backed out of the cargo hold when it was my turn. In a quick minute, I was clear of the harbor and started heading west on Highway Six. I found a payphone at a local gas station just a few minutes after departing the ferry. There was enough room to pull the truck off onto the shoulder and away from the busy road. It was 8 am and time to call work. Becky answered, surprised to hear from me this early in the morning. I told her I was back on the mainland.

"What? You weren't scheduled back until this afternoon."

"Plans changed, and I am back early."

"Did you have an enjoyable trip to Nantucket?"

"No, not really. The foreman arrived just in time to load and go. He had an awful disposition and, if you don't mind, I will pass on the next trip to Nantucket. I never want to step foot on another ferry."

"Well, that's a surprise. I don't have a load for you this early. Start heading west toward Sturbridge, Mass. You can hole up at the truck stop there. I should have a load for you later this afternoon."

"Thank you," I said, then ending the call. Happy as a clam to be off that island.

******

Not all bad guys are men. I was dispatched to pick up a load in Hartford, CT. The place was busy with normal workday stuff. The loader invited me to go inside to the break room and have a coffee; it was free. I thanked him and walked inside. Of course, I visited the restroom and washed up a bit. I walked into a mid-sized breakroom with maybe six oblong tables. There was a half-full coffee pot on the counter with cups and supplies sitting next to it. I poured myself a cup and noticed a well-dressed man sitting by himself, his head in his hands, looking like he was going to cry or die at any moment. I took the initiative and sat across from him with my coffee.

"Are you okay?" I asked, knowing full well he could holler at me for being intrusive.

"Who are you?"

"Oh, I am Patty, a trucker and just killing a few minutes. You seem really upset, what's wrong?"

"I am not okay at all. I need someone to talk to and there isn't anyone here that I can trust."

"I am safe and have big shoulders. Lay it on me," I said with a kind smile.

The man let out a very long sigh. "I have a female colleague who won't leave me alone. It's so bad that I can't even move without her hanging all over me. She is constantly telling me that I could do better than my wife, that I need to take her out, and all that nonsense. She breathes down my neck all day long. If that isn't bad enough, she gags me with too much perfume. Hell, I can smell her before I see her. I dread coming to work."

"Wow, that's some terrible sexual harassment. Where is she right now?"

"I got a break for at least an hour due to a meeting she was called away to attend. She will trot right back the second the meeting ends. Hell, the dumb bitch follows me home and parks in front of my house just to intimidate my wife. It's really that bad! I am newly married to a woman I adore, and we are expecting our first child. To make matters worse, we are deep into an expensive mortgage. What can I do?"

"What does HR say about it?"

"I tried that. The problem is she has two best friends who work in HR. She got the job with zero qualifications. She is dumb as a brick and highly incompetent."

"You need to cut the cord and run. Cut your losses. Send out applications and start over far away."

"She will follow me."

"No, do it in secret. Find somewhere else to work, pack up your home and family without discussing it with anyone. Explain to your new employer the extent of your sexual harassment, and you won't be giving a two-week notice. You can't, or else she will be all over you." The guy perked up.

"I almost forgot something. She is planning a road trip to Miami with her girlfriends next month for a birthday or something." A smile came across his face after he realized that he could possibly escape this madness.

He took a big drink of his coffee, then said, "This could be even better. Every so often, we have strangers come to our door asking us if we are planning to sell. We always say a polite no, but just maybe, that's the perfect solution. I can't wait to go home tonight and talk to my wife."

Just then, the receiver popped his head inside the break room. "Your trailer is loaded, Ma'am."

"Ok, thank you." I stood up to leave, and the guy gave me a firm handshake and a pat on my shoulder.

"Thank you for listening and possibly helping me find a way out."

"My pleasure." I wrote my address down on a napkin. "I want to hear from you. Tell me where you are starting over. I know you can do this! You and your family deserve better. Best of luck to you. Please write to me."

Sure enough, a little over two months later, I received a postcard from Phoenix. He thanked me profusely and said he and his family are settled in their new place and loving it. He said he is receiving a much larger salary for the same work, and the move was so worth it. That made my day and then some.

******

This brief story is a reminder of how often we are unfairly judged. I was in a tiny little town in the middle of Nebraska with not much more than a stop light or two. I needed to reference my map. There was a gas station with a big enough lot to pull off and park my rig. It didn't take five minutes before a car screeched up next to me. An angry woman got out and stomped up to my door. She screamed that I was sleeping with her husband and asked how dare I show my face in town. She was sputtering and hollering, acting completely unhinged. I rolled my window down about halfway.

"Ma'am, I only stopped here to check my map. I live several states away, and I assure you I don't know a living soul here. If you're this upset over a woman driver, you have bigger problems than I can fix."

She gave me a deer-in-the-headlights look, sputtered a few more incoherent things, then drove away. She left me shaking my head.

~ ~

Chapter Thirteen

Good Guys

I severely broke my hand. Nobody could have seen this coming. It was nobody's fault, just an unfortunate event. It was the summer of my third year working for Ron. Several of us were given a new truck. They were higher-end Freightliners with power steering. We ran 350 Cummins engines and 6-speed manual transmissions. The fact that it had power steering made all the difference in me being able to continue working or not. This is what happened:

My first dispatch with my new ride was to a company in the middle of Iowa. Once a week, we would bring them a load of parts, drop the trailer in their dock, and pick up the empty from the previous drop-off. It wasn't a big company, they only had three docks. The signed bills from the previous load were in the empty trailer, so we normally didn't have contact with a receiver. I arrived on the morning of a gorgeous summer day, and it couldn't have been more perfect.

The company looked deserted, but then again, most did unless it was break time or shift change. I backed into the empty dock, set only my trailer brakes, and then backed up tight to the trailer before setting my tractor brakes. This actually takes the pressure off of the fifth-wheel release pin, making it easier to pull. Most drivers use a pull bar to reach the handle of the pin because it's pretty far underneath the trailer. I am ready to unhook; the dollies are down, and the cords are unhooked. I gave a hard yank on my pin with my pull bar and instead of the pin snapping out; I go backward hard, actually flipping over, ass over applecart. This is where the fun began. I sat up, realizing that both my left hand and pull bar were pinned underneath me. There was a searing pain in my hand, and I absolutely knew that I had just crushed it. The parking lot was warm from the sun, and the heat felt good radiating up. It felt comforting, and I seriously didn't want to move, but I had to. I sat still a minute longer before I rolled up slightly to remove my pin puller and left hand from underneath me. The pain was severe. I held my hand while watching an angry red hematoma form near my wrist. As best as I could tell, my middle and ring fingers were broken, along with a few other central bones. It hurt too much to cry. I knew I couldn't just sit here and feel sorry for myself.

My brain is weirdly hard-wired to fix things. A definitive male trait, but I am not a man, and I absolutely couldn't fix this. I just couldn't fix or wish away my smashed hand. Another minute passed, and then I went up to the door and rang the buzzer.

In a moment, an employee greeted me, "May I help you?"

"Yes, please. If you could send a maintenance man out here, that would be great."

"Um, okay, let me find someone for you."

"Thank you."

Not even two minutes later, this big, brawny hero of a guy came out. "What seems to be the problem, ma'am?"

"I am having a bit of a problem unhooking and took a nasty fall." I showed him my hand.

"Holy crap! Do you need a hospital or something?"

"Yes, and no. Actually, for now, I just need a bit of help to pull my pin."

"Let me try," he said, really looking unsure. Kind of like he was thinking of tossing me in his car to get me some medical help. He took my puller and gave it a very hard yank. It didn't budge. He gave it a much harder yank, and that released it.

"Thank you so very much. I can't even believe how tight that was." I said, relieved.

"That took every bit of strength I had. You need to go back to your terminal and have that fixed."

"Yes, that's my plan, but I have to make a pick up on my way back."

"You're not seriously going to try to drive, are you?"

"Driving will be the easy part. It's my left hand."

He took a minute to help me hook to the empty trailer. After he knew I was all set to leave, he bid me farewell. "Well, good luck, miss," he said, sounding almost apologetic.

My hand and wrist looked like a red and purple baseball mitt. I needed to find splints and a wrap soon. I motored east with my hand gingerly resting on my steering wheel. It was painful.

There was a big truck stop called Iowa 80 a little over an hour from my location. I pulled in and got fuel with the help of a driver at the fuel island next to me. I thanked him and then parked. My plan was to go inside and find someone with a kind heart. I slipped my roll of black electrical tape into my pocket to secure the splints, if I could figure that part out. After washing my hands, I looked at the damage and thought that I might be totally screwed. I walked around and then stood at the edge of the restaurant. My stomach started growling, reminding me that my last meal was yesterday. It was noon.

I spotted a guy at a table in the far corner with a cup of coffee, looking bored. He was clean shaven, had short dark brown hair, and he was wearing a blue polo shirt. Maybe a driver, maybe not. I walked over to him and smiled, feeling out of place.

"Do you have a moment to help me figure out something?" He looked at me, a bit startled.

"Sure, sit down. What can I help you with?"

"I have a bit of a problem." I showed him my hand, and he had a fit.

"Jesus' miss! You really busted your hand. Holy crap, when did this happen?"

"A few hours ago. I got a new truck, and the pin was a bit tight. The result was my hand got severely broken. I need help to figure out a splint and a wrap."

He held my hand, looking it over. He was really hurting me, but I put on a brave face.

"Okay, I think we can get this figured out. I still have an hour left on my break. I have an idea. Wait here."

He came back with two washed off sticks from ice-cream bars. He had cut them in half, so four splints and a clean rag and a pair of scissors that he must have borrowed from somewhere. I didn't want to know where the sticks came from. At least they were clean. I pulled the tape out of my pocket, and he went to work. He quickly straightened out my two fingers, which took all my power not to scream. I couldn't stop the tears. He apologized, then set them with sticks and tape. Then he skillfully cut the clean rag into strips and wrapped my hand.

"Your hand is demolished. It's going to be about three months before you are truly alright again."

"How did you wrap my hand so skillfully?"

He laughed at that. "Well, I was an emergency room tech while in college. I have wrapped up a lot of damaged parts."

"Why are you a trucker and not a doctor?" I asked.

At that moment, he looked like he was just run over by his own truck. His expression was so sad.

He said, "Life happens." I didn't ask any further and also decided not to talk about my nursing school background. It wasn't relevant.

"Thank you so very much for helping me."

"You're welcome. You will be alright. Just try not to bang it too much. There isn't really anything else you can do except let it heal. Seriously, it will take three months."

He got up and left, bidding me a nice farewell. I told him, "Thanks, and drive safe."

The server saw me alone. She brought me a glass of water and two Tylenol. "I was kind of watching you, and that looks painful. Are you hungry? Can I get you anything?"

"Yes, I would really like a bowl of soup and a sandwich, please. You choose. I can't put two thoughts together right now."

"Okay," she said with a big smile.

She brought me a steaming bowl of chicken noodle soup and an open-faced turkey sandwich with mashed potatoes and gravy. It was a lot of food. The entire time eating, I kept going over why the pin was so tight. It made no sense. I finished eating, paid for my food, and left her a decent tip.

After eating, all I wanted to do was sleep. I made my way outside and felt disoriented. The sun was in my eyes, and I momentarily forgot where I had parked my rig. After a minute or so, I remembered that I had parked in a corner spot away from everyone. I climbed into my cab, closed my curtains, and then peeled my clothes off using my right hand and my left thumb. This seemed to be the only working part of my left hand. The Tylenol was effective, and I fell asleep with my last thoughts spinning around how difficult the next three months would be.

The next morning, I made my pick up at a company in the Chicago suburbs. The receiver instantly noticed my wrapped hand, and he helped me secure my doors open before I backed in, and then he closed me up and put the seal on when I was done. He was worried about me and told me to see a doctor.

I nodded and thanked him for his assistance. I was there less than an hour in total.

I reached the terminal later that afternoon. I parked in the loaded line and walked into the shop. I politely asked Eli, the new mechanic, if he could pull my pin.

"Do you seriously need help with that? You're in a brand-new truck."

"The pin is so tight that I fell and busted my hand trying to pull it."

I showed him the bandaged-up baseball mitt pretending to be my left hand.

"Oh, jeez, ouch, that looks really sore. So sorry I was making fun of you. That doesn't look good."

He followed me to my rig, then he casually reached under the trailer, grabbed the pin, and gave it a yank. It didn't budge. He yanked it again, even harder. No go. Then he asked me for my puller and gave it an even harder yank, and it released, nearly knocking him backward.

"Damn. Wow. Finish dropping your trailer and bring it into the shop. I will adjust your fifth wheel and loosen your pin to where it belongs."

"Thank you." I brought the truck to the shop. After that, I walked over to the driver's room. It was a beautiful day, and the door was propped open. Larry, who has been the day dispatcher for a while now, didn't like cigarette smoke. Everyone is breathing easier these days with the influx of fresh air. The first thing I noticed was Ron talking to Steve, Roger, and a couple of others. He immediately saw my hand.

"Sit down and explain," Ron demanded, looking worried.

So, all of us sat down together, and I went through the entire story from the beginning. Ron carefully took my hand and began to remove the rag bandage. My hand was heavily swollen with red and purple stripes, and the hematoma at my wrist was still full of blood.

Ron whistled in disbelief, "Looks like you demolished your hand. How did you even get the truck back here?"

"Driving isn't difficult. It's everything else that's a challenge. I can't write with my right hand, so unfortunately, Eleanor will need to learn Chinese."

Everyone laughed at that. Ron got out a fancy first aid kit. He kept the electrical tape and splints in place, then he tried to re-wrap my hand with real gauze.

"You know Patty, I should take you for x-rays."

"Thanks Ron, but we're past the point of no return. There isn't much a doctor can do besides tell me it's broken. I will be careful, and it will heal up on its own."

"I suppose you're right. Hell, we all get busted up. We blow the dust off and keep going."

"Exactly," I answered.

Roger told Ron to step aside, he could do a better job wrapping. Roger didn't like the splints or the wrap, so I kindly explained that, for now, it was the best that could be done.

"The splints can stay, at least for the time being," Roger said. Then, he expertly wrapped my hand back up with real gauze. It hurt so bad to have my hand checked over, manipulated, and so forth, but I had to suck it up.

Everyone gathered around me and told their own stories. Roger said he had a lot of combat stories, but he took a pass because he didn't want his nightmares to start back up. Steve said he stubbed his big toe on his nightstand, and it hurt for a week. Leroy was there and told us about falling off his pony as a kid, which broke his collarbone. Everyone was doing their best to lighten the mood and make me feel better.

The biggest surprise came when Billy came in with his pronounced limp. He must have heard us before he walked in.

"Y'all know that I used to run a cattle business with my dad. We worked together for years, and I never figured I would ever do anything else. Ever' so often, we would take a trailer load of cows to the meat processing plant. This was just part of the business. So, on no particular day, I was off-loading cattle at the plant, and something spooked the heifer I was about to guide down the ramp. She flared up and rammed hard against my leg, pinning me against the door frame.

Then, a second heifer got all riled up and rammed into her. I nearly blacked out from the pain she inflicted. I was taken to the hospital. She broke my leg in four places and dislocated my hip. Nothing healed right, and I never felt safe enough to continue that job. Dad understood and hired a couple of hands to help out. I felt terrible. This was a decade ago, and I still have problems."

Nobody spoke for a minute. Billy had never opened up to anyone, and we were taken by surprise.

"Wow, Billy. Thank you for sharing this. We never knew what had happened to you," Ron said thoughtfully. We all talked to him, showing an abundance of care and concern. Billy shoved Roger over and sat next to me. He picked up my hand and said,

"Everything will work out. You will heal." I was so close to tears at this point from everything, the stress, the trauma, the intense pain, and the thoughtfulness of the guys I had become close to. Good guys down to the core.

Ron spoke up. "I am sending you home, Patty. Your hand needs a few days to settle down. You can go out on Sunday if you feel up to it."

"Thank you, Ron."

I had a tough three months. Everyone was right about that timeline. I was able to continue working, but I had some real challenges. Winter hurt, I bought a big fuzzy mitten to wear on that hand and that helped. My biggest challenge was opening the side box. That required my left hand to pull and hold a cable behind my driver's seat while my right hand lifted up the side box door. I ended up keeping a lot of my tools and stuff in the passenger side of my cab. It took a long time before I had the strength in my hand to pull that cable. Past that, I dealt with everything else as best as I could. And yes, I managed to bang my hand on everything it seemed. By the following spring, I was completely healed.

******

The good guys are in abundance. They are the ones who pull off the highway behind you, not knowing who you are, but stopping anyway just to help. They will try to fix your truck, if possible, whether it's a brake adjustment or any of a million other things. These guys will try to help. They will help when you are lost, or when our loads become unstable, such as flatbed loads. I could go on and on about how big our hearts are. Good guys help folks with car trouble and flat tires too. It's a long list of good deeds.

******

Somewhere in the early 1990s, I was picking up a load at a foundry. I was bone weary, and tired. As soon as I got there and was checked in, the receiver had me back in. He told me it would be a couple of hours before I would be loaded. It was probably 90 degrees on the dock, if not hotter. I didn't care, all I wanted was a nap. After about an hour of dead, beautiful sleep, I was awoken by someone literally picking me up and carrying me out of the truck. He was a stranger who thought I was going to get heat stroke or something. He said he regularly picks up at that foundry and the receiver mentioned a female sleeping.

"How come you woke me up?" I asked, not fully awake."

"Well, miss. It's too dang hot for a nap. You weren't safe to sleep in this kind of heat."

He propped me up on my feet fully expecting gratitude. "Ummm okay, thanks I guess."

He disappeared, so I climbed right back into my bunk. This time, I locked the door and fell right back to sleep. It was about two hours later when the receiver tapped on my door to let me know I was loaded. There was no sign of the stranger. He was a good guy. He meant well.

******

A bit later in my career, I was sent to a manufacturing company that had an abundance of security. Not a big deal. I pulled up to the guard shack and was greeted by a sweet man who had Down syndrome. I was proud of him for getting that job, and he seemed competent. We get chatting about things and he casually mentioned wanting to take me home.

He said, "It's too dangerous for a girl to be out here all by herself. I can take care of you. My apartment is tiny, but I promise you will be loved and cared for. I will make you safe."

I responded with a big smile, "Thank you for being so sweet. I do alright for a girl alone."

"No, really, I insist. When you get done in there, park over there in the grass where I can find you."

He was pointing to a spot where a truck wouldn't fit. I couldn't fault his sweetness, but it was highly misplaced. He opened the gate, and I drove down a long driveway to a building. I checked in and so on. It took about an hour to get loaded and I was beginning to stress about the guard. I wasn't sure he was going to let me back out. The grassy area was inside the gate. So, after loading and all that, I needed to leave, and I proceeded towards the gate. To my surprise, it was a different guard. It was 11:30 am and figured it must have been lunch break. I zoomed out of there. The guard with Down syndrome was a good guy. He had a huge heart.

The End

~ ~

Epilogue

A snapshot of what the future has brought to the industry regarding safety:

The FMCSA (Federal Motor Carrier Safety Administration) made hard rules about rest breaks and companies were shut down right and left for ignoring this. Compliance became mandatory. We must take a ten-hour rest break at the end of our workday and a thirty-minute break during our workday. The days of forced driving ended long ago. Bottom line, we aren't fatigued.

Our trucks today are rolling computers with enough technology to damn near go to the moon and back. We are all much safer with lane controls, disc brakes, adaptive cruise control and GPS, which is the best thing ever invented, making paper maps irrelevant for a driver needing directions. This technology also allows companies to pinpoint their equipment with postage stamp precision.

Most trucks now are equipped with forward-facing cameras. This has already saved the trucking industry billions of dollars in needless lawsuits and litigation. Big greedy law firms can't profit off of crashes anymore. We are cleared or convicted based on actual footage and not assumptions. Cars used to hit us on purpose and win because we were the big, bad truck.

Right about 2010, electronic logs were coming around and were soon mandated. Paper logbooks have become nonexistent unless your e-log has an issue, and the company must fix the issue within seven days. We cannot stay on paper logs.

Trucks are comfortable too. Many of us have built in mini-refrigerators and microwaves. Luxury seats and air-ride are so comfortable that we glide along instead of being beaten half to death by springs and junk equipment. Trucking went from stone age to space age within a 40-year span.

~ ~

www.ingramcontent.com/pod-product-compliance
Lightning Source LLC
LaVergne TN
LVHW010119090726
842905LV00039B/934
9798230019312